LINKS OF LIFE

Links of Life

by Joe Kirkwood

as told to BARBARA FEY

Introduction by **LOWELL THOMAS**

Foreword by Barbara Fey

Library of Congress Catalog Card Number: 73–2008
Copyright 1973 by Ronald R. Kirkwood. First edition.
Manufactured in the U.S.A.

INTRODUCTION
By Lowell Thomas

Although Joe Kirkwood was proud to be an American, he never lost his enthusiasm for his native Australia. I suppose I knew him longer than any of his host of American friends and fans. More than half a century ago I first met Joe. It was in Melbourne, and although in his teens he was a local hero, amateur golf champion of the Land Down Under. It was Joe who gave me my first golf lesson. It happened this way:

After a run at the Century Theater and Madison Square Garden in New York, followed by a record season at Covent Garden Opera House and Royal Albert Hall in London, Australia's colorful Prime Minister Billy Hughes had invited me to the Antipodes. This was because in my film and story of the Palestine and Arabian campaign the Australian Light Horse and the Anzac Mounted Division played a dramatic role. The Prime Minister, wanting to get us off to a flying start, had asked me to appear before a joint session of the Australian Parliament. He also had arranged for Australia's number-one World War I military personality, Sir John Monash, to give a luncheon in honor of my wife and myself. Across the table sat a genial gentleman who was introduced as a previous amateur golf champion. When he found out that I had never played the game, he offered to take me around what then was the best-known course in the country, the Melbourne Metropolitan. With some coaching from him I managed to survive the round, and even did better than an eminent member of the foursome ahead of us. Cyril Maude, a famous British actor, back at the clubhouse locker room, told us he had lost sixteen balls.

At any rate, as a result of my first round I was bitten by the bug and a day or two later took my first lesson. My mentor was none other than Australia's sensational new champion, young Joe Kirkwood.

During the following decade all I knew about Joe was that he had left Australia and had been playing as a touring pro and giving exhibitions in Europe and America. Then, when we settled on a farm in Dutchess County, New York, we invited Joe to pay us a visit. From then on he spent a week or two with us every year.

At an early age Joe had left home and gone to work on a South Australia sheep station. There he got his first glimpse of golf, shagging balls for his boss. When the latter discovered that the lad had an aptitude for the game, he backed him and entered him in local tournaments. Within a few years Joe was the amateur champion.

Physically Joe was one of the most powerful men I ever knew. He could hit the ball farther with a seven iron than I could with a driver.

Joe Kirkwood also was a man of many talents. Even though he had hardly any schooling, one of his hobbies was geology. Over the years as he traveled back and forth giving golf exhibitions across America, he made a collection of stones. A hundred or more of these he himself polished superbly. Then he fitted them together for a coffee tabletop which for years was conspicuous in my New York City office and excited much admiration.

In addition to his collection of stones Joe's car was loaded with fishing rods and other gear. As a fisherman he had few peers. During the days he visited us each year, he would spend more time fishing than playing golf. Then in the evening he would tell us stories of his travels, especially the years when he and the one-and-only Walter Hagen toured the world together. Some of those stories, fortunately, are recorded in this book.

The first time Richard Nixon ran for vice-president, he and Mrs. Nixon came to Quaker Hill to spend a weekend with Governor and Mrs. Thomas E. Dewey. Following a visit to our home four of us played a round of golf. The other in the foursome was Joe Kirkwood. Coming down the seventh fairway and following some frustrating shots, Mr. Nixon apologetically remarked how he had only attempted golf a few times. Said Governor Dewey: "Dick, here you are with one of the most famous of all golf pros. Why not get some advice from him?" Which he did. And I assume that was when the man later destined to be our president had his first golf lesson. Since then he has been enough of an enthusiast to put several practice fairways and greens on the grounds of the Western White House at San Clemente.

One day after a round of golf, the day Joe made an eagle five on the longest hole in the world, I said, "Joe, you recall President Wilson's famous Fourteen Points which he believed could lead to world peace? How about summing up golf in the same way?" Whereupon he dictated the following which I have framed on the wall of our locker room:—

JOE KIRKWOOD'S 14 POINTS

1. Relax, relax, relax!

2. When addressing ball, stand almost straight, sitting back slightly on your heels.

3. Extend hands, arms and club out straight. That is, don't drop your hands as though putting them in your lap.

4. Grip should always be the same. If you want a hook or a fade, a low shot or a high one simply alter your stance.

5. For instance if you want a high shot, open your club face and stand behind the ball.

6. Get biggest arc possible. Slow backswing. Slight hesitation at top.

7. Stay almost flat footed through swing until after ball is in flight and clubhead is out where it should be on the follow through. It's okay to sway a little as you pivot, but your head must not move too much. On your pivot be sure to bring left shoulder way under.

8. Imagine you are looking underneath the ball. Avoid closing club face.

9. Whatever you do don't let your body get ahead of your hands and the club.

10. Don't fight the wind. For example, on the Quaker Hill course, in playing the 7th where the wind often is from the West, hit a fade to the left and allow wind to bring the ball around. This way you will get more distance.

11. On pitch and chip shots keep arms stiff. Arms, hands, club all one piece.

12. On pitch and chip shots use slow easy rhythmical stroke, with a follow through. Don't snap at the ball!

13. In rough, or any bad lie, open club face in order to cut through trouble.

14. In getting out of traps spank the sand with club head. Use light touch; easy stroke. Don't bang at it. After rain, or in any hard sand, use a very light touch; caress it.

Relax! Be Loose! But not loose as a goose.

Joe Kirkwood for several years was a member of the American Golf Hall of Fame Selection Committee, of which I was chairman. Along with the veteran Scottish pro, George Ferrier, Robert Trent Jones, and several others, here was the first group to be honored by the Golf Hall of Fame:—

Harry Vardon	Henry Cotton
J. H. Taylor	Joyce Weathered
James Braid	Gene Sarazen
Francis Ouimet	Tommy Armour
Robert Tyre Jones	Sam Snead
Walter Hagen	Ben Hogan
Charles "Chick" Evans	Byron Nelson
	"Babe" Zaharias

A year or two later I was much pleased when my colleagues unanimously agreed that Joe Kirkwood also should be included in the American Hall of Fame. I suspect that he did more to popularize golf than any other man who ever lived. This book tells part of the story.

FOREWORD

By Barbara Fey

Joe Kirkwood was born April 3, 1897, in Sydney, Australia, fittingly enough on Fore Street. Throughout his life he held his humble bush-boy beginnings dear to his heart and memories. At the age of ten, Joe left his home and walked more than 370 miles through the hills and lowlands of his country to reach the sheep station of a friendly sponsor, J. R. Sellar. He walked alone, without compass, map, or watch, following the rivers and woods, guiding his way with the help of a railroad timetable by mentally clocking the movements of freight trains with the sun above.

His experiences as a drover lad—riding the fence lines, learning to live in solitude with nature and yet to get along with his fellow man—all had their foundation there on the ranch, and these were the tools of his education.

By strange chance the owner of this spread was a golf enthusiast and had Joe set up a makeshift three-hole course on some pastureland for passing the time during idle evenings. The young drover made his own clubs, forming the heads and shafts from saplings and using snakeskin for the grips. He became fascinated and preoccupied with the game of golf, and when he entered and won his first tournament at the age of sixteen, nobody could have been more surprised and elated. From that day forward he worked with inspiration and determination to understand every facet of the game and to perfect his playing abilities.

Joe first came to America in 1921 on his way to England. His spirit of generosity in performing before wounded servicemen in his native country was inspiration for a repertoire of amusing golfing feats. These he demonstrated for the entertainment of the participants in a tournament in Pinehurst, North Carolina. Strangely, this set the stage for his future career because, although he had won all the Australian titles and had gone on to Europe to win many more, he was strongly influenced by a series of premeditated foul plays set against him during his first try at international competition.

He had fared very well in the practice rounds and was on his way to winning the British Open at St. Andrews when the bookies and bettors toppled him. With the lack of control over the gallery crowds in those days, his ball was surreptitiously moved and trampled on; noise came inopportunely from the spectators with more than coincidence during putts and stroke play. And on the final round, when he was well within the winner's circle, a man yelled an obscenity during the back swing of his drive, causing Joe to falter and slip his shot off line. The ball hit a spectator full face, injuring him badly and frightening Joe so much that finishing the round became a dull nightmare. There was such a quantity of money riding on the outcome of the match that the bookmakers couldn't afford to let the newcomer win and had set out to sabotage the tournament, which they did.

The affair disillusioned and undermined the young man's

goals and dreams. He became hard-put to see whether there was any value in winning under such circumstances and took a different look at his life and future. Chance turned up an invitation to play his exhibition of trick shots and golf wizardry before some highborn personages. Among them were the king and queen of England, who invited him to become their instructor, whereupon the young man turned pro of a different sort.

He was wined and dined all over Europe by gatherings from every rank. When he returned to America en route to his native Australia and was approached by the famous Walter Hagen to enter a joint exhibition tour, Joe felt that the die was cast. Together this team played 125 four-ball matches in the next six months, traveling from coast to coast, a record never approached by any golf team, American or foreign.

For the next three years these two partnered on a circuit that took them around the world, to golf courses and galleries of every land. They were entertained by kings and queens, sultans and maharajas, settlers and natives of a world and era now past. An age of discovery for the literate, an age of exploitation for some, but still an age when they halted a war—called a stop to hostilities between the Chinese and Japanese—to see Joe Kirkwood and Walter Hagen put on their golf show.

Joe toured later with Gene Sarazen, then reteamed for many years with Hagen, finally settling down to become resident pro at the Huntingdon Valley Golf Club outside Philadelphia, still teaching and giving his exhibition. He never seriously reentered tournament play, feeling that the pressures were too great and the money too little and that his approach to golf that used so many ways to hit a shot interfered with competitive concentration. Yet over the years he beat every one of the name "greats" ever on the tour, before there was a tour.

Joe had twenty-nine holes-in-one to his golfing credit, including one played off the face of a man's watch during an exhibition at Cedar Rapids, Iowa, and another earned while Grantland Rice's news cameramen were shooting a golf movie at Sea Island, Georgia. He even shot two holes-in-one during a single round of play. He was the first pro ever to use the wooden golf tee as we know it today. Before Joe took up the Reddy Tee, small mounds of sand and water were patted together and placed on the ground for the drive shot. He developed and improved the manufacture of present-day golf clubs, working as an adviser to Golfcraft engineers, and he contributed his lifetime-knowledge of the sport to others as a teaching pro.

The final years of Joe Kirkwood's life were spent in the rolling green hills of Stowe, Vermont, where once again he was pro, friend, entertainer, a man's man, and a monumental human being.

CONTENTS

ILLUSTRATIONS

Hagen teaching natives to shimmy
Hagen shooting crap with natives
A Tanganyika "caddie"
Kirkwood in India
Kirkwood in Celon
Kirkwood at Madras, India
Hagen in India
One of Kirkwood's trick shots
Kirkwood in Egypt
Hagen and Kirkwood racing around a pyramid
A Bali native girl
The Bali home of Le Mare
Le Mare's Balinese housemaid
A Balinese golf lesson
Kirkwood practicing in Bali
Kirkwood teaching golf to Japanese soldiers
Hagen and Kirkwood in Hungjao, China
Hagen and Kirkwood in Miyanoshita, Japan
The first tee, Ibaraki, Japan
Hagen in the early 1940's
Kirkwood entertaining the Duke and Duchess of
    Windsor in the Bahamas
Kirkwood on his way to England
An exhibition in England
An exhibition at San Quentin Prison
Kirkwood entertaining servicemen in Atlanta, Georgia
A golf exhibition in Pennsylvania
Kirkwood imitating a beginner
Kirkwood hitting three balls in an exhibition
Kirkwood's bag of clubs
Kirkwood's tombstone

PART ONE

EXHIBITIONS—THE CROSSROADS OF MY LIFE

Many people have asked me how I got started doing my exhibition, where it all began. Actually, while still in Australia I had done some entertaining for servicemen wounded while fighting in World War I. I had given some of my free time to these men, but they had taught me too. In preparing a "show" for them, I fooled around to see if I could hit the ball standing on one leg, also controlling the ball with just a single arm, either one of them. This was all to demonstrate that these men could recover and regain health and have some fun too. However, it also developed in me the ability to really analyze the stroke and balance of golf and learn how to compensate, skills that were to benefit me later, both in tournament play and in the amusing part of the act I developed.

It was never my intention to make exhibition material the main breadwinner of my life—it happened quite by accident. I had left Australia for my first competition abroad and traveled to Europe via the United States. I had heard of Pinehurst and planned to stop there for some experience.

There were several tournaments being played there including the North and South Championship.

To my surprise, I received an invitation to play and found that I was drawn against none other than Walter Hagen. They teamed us together for all four rounds, and even more incredible was the fact that we finished with identical scores. This elated me tremendously, for Walter was at the height of his fame. Furthermore, we played on sand greens, which was a first in my book and set me back quite a bit, since learning the speed of the new surface took a special knack.

Following the tournament play on Sunday, they usually had an exhibition for the spectators and contestants too. They'd heard that I'd done some work for the veterans back home, and they called on me to help out with the show. I naturally agreed. It was for no reason at all, just for the entertainment of the guests at the hotel, and I was amazed by the crowd of people that gathered to watch. Perhaps it was the beautiful sunny afternoon, but certainly a large group arranged themselves around, making a horseshoe circle with many seated and others standing.

Halfway through the show they stopped for an announcement; some prominent man rose and gave a speech. I think that it was Mayor Jimmy Walker of New York, but all I can remember him saying was, "Folks, this lad has come a long way to entertain you all, and I think it's up to us to show our appreciation." Someone started up a collection then and there, and presented it to me with good wishes for my future success. I was stunned. The amount was a staggering $770, including several fifty-dollar bills. Most important to me was the fact that in this group of people were all the pros who had assembled for the tournament. I felt it was quite an honor that they had enjoyed my country wit and humor, and antic shots.

The person who was even more impressed by all that instant money turned out to be my opponent and new acquaintance, Walter Hagen. When Walter saw all that green gathered after one short "show," he couldn't wait to come to my side and suggest getting together in the future. It was indeed the crossroads of my life when "the Haig" invited me to team up for some exhibition golf following my trip to England. At the time I didn't give it much thought, but it was the real start of our long friendship and the embryo of our business relationship too. Little did I know that, following that one demonstration, I would receive letters and telegrams from all over America inviting me to appear before golfing groups and clubs. It was quite a challenging thought, and although I was committed to proceed to England, I agreed to return.

Months later, back in America, Walter and I set up a format, playing thirty-six holes against the local pros or amateurs—eighteen in the morning, eighteen in the afternoon—and my hour-long show following the matches. As it worked out, during our first stint we played 105 exhibitions in 109 days. Of course that was before there was any golf tournament circuit as there is today, with large purses and huge audiences. At that time Walter and I struck the most lucrative arrangement ever made in golf. Our travel expenses were great to be sure, but admission charges gave us a nice fee, and we saw a lot of the world, people from every walk of life, and places and sights then known to only a few travelers. In fact, we felt that these were the "links of life," and we were on our way to seeing and living them all.

GREAT DAY FOR AUSTRALIA

Following the early years of my boyhood, my ranching boss, J. R. Sellar, awakened an interest in me in the sport of golf. It grew with each hour of practice and culminated during my first tournament. I longed to be different from my contemporaries; I wanted to be better, the best at something. That something, for me, was definitely golf.

It was Mr. Sellar who arranged for me to serve my five years' apprenticeship to the pro at the Manly Course in my native Sydney (the salary, five shillings a week, about one dollar). And it was again this fine man who later made it possible for me to move on to another club as pro. I was playing during that period too, and I beat just about everyone. It became clear that I had a career developing before me, with scores of 66, 68, 67 played with the rather primitive equipment we had then. The real proof, however, lay in the fact that I won everything going—all the professional and amateur competitions, including the New Zealand Professional and Open and the Australian Open, the first time I entered them.

The older golfers decided to send me to England to St. Andrews and the British championships. They set up a fund for my travel expenses and hoped I would represent them well.

At that time, like all youngsters, I had an idol. He was Harry Vardon of England; this man was truly the greatest, for me a god. He won the British Golf Championship six times as well as countless other honors, and anything I could get to read about Vardon I scrambled for; any pictures, information, and tips were like nectar to me. I molded my game around Vardon's, trying to imitate his every movement, and studied all that I could of his technique, his swing, his timing, and even his thinking.

When I arrived in England, I found that there was a tournament scheduled at Gleneagles, Scotland, before the Open Championship. Thirty-two players could qualify, which I did most easily with a 70 and a 71. It was to be match play for the actual tournament, and miraculously I was drawn to oppose Harry Vardon for my first contest. Though I couldn't help being elated, I was also scared to death. In fact, I went to the tee shaking like a leaf, but I found Vardon to be extremely charming and gracious. Of course he didn't know how thrilled I was, a raw rookie playing against my idol. Luckily my caddie sensed my nervousness and didn't let me hurry too quickly to the tee.

We started down the fairway smartly with quite a group looking on. Vardon, splitting the greensward down the middle, was relentlessly accurate on every shot. Feeling ten feet off the ground, I found myself more engrossed with his ball than mine, and more watchful of his swing and stance than my own. Gleneagles is located in Perthshire, and its gently rolling fairways were bordered then by purple heather and masses of golden broom. Truly it would have been a sight

7

for the eyes to feast upon if it hadn't been for the seriousness of the match.

Turning my mind from both the glories of the scenery and the exhilaration of my competition, I tried to settle down and spot some weakness in my opponent's game. From the offset, his soft spot seemed to be only on the green. I remember that it began on the very first hole, where Vardon took three putts and should have lost, but even though he laid me a stymie, we halved it. Another three putts followed at the second hole, and just to vary the monotony, he actually took four on the third green, missing one no longer than the length of a pipe stem.

On the seventh I really demoralized him by taking out my homemade mashie (my seven clubs, two woods, four irons and a putter were all self-made) and, planting my feet deep in the bunker, cut across the ball with a whiplike action. It flew to the left, and, on contact with the ground, the ball broke swiftly at right angles and finished not far from the cup.

As the match progressed, my fortunes held unbelievably well. On the fourteenth, Vardon was only one down, and then an astounding thing happened. This was a long one-shot hole of 245 yards, with pleasant hills bordering either side of the green. Vardon was nicely on with his tee shot, six yards from the hole. I lay two and was a foot from the pin. On the line of Vardon's putt was an insinuating little hollow. The ball ran through the hollow, skipped merrily down the other side and ran on and on past the hole, ending behind mine in a dead stymie. Vardon had incredibly stymied himself and had to settle for halving a hole that he should have won!

By the eighteenth we had squared the match and had to go out again. The first hole, 355 yards, in ordinary circumstances was a drive and an easy mashie shot, but this day a gale wind and spluttering rain stretched it to two full shots. Vardon played a brassie for his second and was short, so short that the ball almost trickled back into the bunker. This was certainly an opening for me. Following my drive, I decided on a long iron, low into the wind, and I carried the hill, landing my ball only eight yards from the pin. Vardon chipped well on, but was still short of an easy putt, so although my ball looked miles away to me, I was there in two to his three.

I knew this was *it*. I didn't mind the thought of losing, but I wanted to give a good showing for the friends back home who had had such faith in me. With the adrenalin pumping, I grasped my putter with a strong right-hand grip, opened my stance and looked right at the hole. Arms close to my body, I stroked through, following with the club head, and darned if I didn't sink it!

A bit surprised, Vardon turned to me grinning and said, "Joe, that was very rude of you!" I was so flabbergasted that I couldn't even talk.

In the afternoon I drew a young player, the ranking English star at the time, Arthur Havers. He was a big man, near six foot four, and hit a very long ball. Every shot off the tee outdistanced mine by about seventy yards, which made him feel pretty complacent. But my second shots were often inside his ball, which he didn't seem to notice. The match went to the twentieth hole, but I won it too.

What an introduction to international golf! I couldn't believe that I'd succeeded the first time I had played away from my native country. Surely it was a great day for Australia and all those who had sent me across the oceans and continents. A great day for Australia, and a great day for a young man who had dreams and hopes, but never imagined triumph would come so suddenly.

9

EMBARRASSING MOMENTS

Following the tournament at Gleneagles, I journeyed south to England. Naturally, my first move was to post my entry to an important local tournament before the Open. (I was a registered member of the British PGA.) Upon going down to find my starting time, however, I found that the authorities hadn't registered me. I wasn't even listed and they wouldn't allow me to play.

The newspapers had so influenced the officials with their criticism before they had seen me, intimating that I was making a mockery of the sport, that I was stopped before I started. The press literally tore me apart, saying that I was burlesquing and buffooning their hallowed game of golf.

Following this rebuff, I was booked to play an exhibition at Selden Park Golf Club just outside London. It so happened that the day before I received by courier a rather important-looking letter with the British Royal Crest on the envelope, requesting me to give an exhibition Saturday for the royal family at Sir Philip Sassoon's estate at Trent. On that particular day, however, I was already scheduled for a show elsewhere. This engagement had been definitely confirmed some weeks earlier, and I sent my reply by telegram addressing it to the king's aide: "Sincerely regret not available Saturday. Will gladly arrange to appear Sunday."

When I arrived at the club near noon and the committee learned of this letter and my refusal to play for royalty, all hell broke loose. Both the members and the committee seemed deeply concerned and astonished, and tried to explain to me that such a request constituted a "royal command." Therefore one must accept and obey, passing all other engagements, particularly since I was a British subject from Australia.

They immediately suggested my calling off the exhibition, counseling, "You jolly well can't do that sort of thing over here!" But a date's a date in my book, and I didn't intend to disappoint all those hundreds of spectators waiting out there and proceeded with my entertainment as planned. Upon hearing this, the newspapers became both more curious and more hostile toward my act, but I wouldn't give them the satisfaction of seeing me and migrated back to Scotland, where I was warmly greeted by all.

Several years later when this old hurt had dimmed, I received a casual invitation from the very same Sir Philip Sassoon to give a program. This time I headed my footsteps toward Trent, a bit richer and perhaps wiser regarding the customs of the land.

I arrived quite late that night. It was nearly two in the morning, and the butler didn't want to let me in. But after I told him my name he commented, "By Jove, you are tardy, Mr. Kirkwood. We expected you here before this."

I agreed that I was a bit off schedule, but joked that I'd come a long way: "Across the sea from Australia."

With the proverbial "By Jove," he set me down to a delicious late supper of hot tea and muffins, complete with Devonshire honey, after which he packed me off to my room for some much-needed sleep.

My accommodation was more like the bridal suite at the Savoy, especially the bed. The beds in England were wonderful anyway. This one, though, was particularly so, warm and soft, like down on a baby bird. Whether it was the bed or just me, that night I was restless and didn't sleep much. However, looking out my window very early the next morning, I saw a sight so glorious that only a paddock full of peacocks could have surpassed it. A blaze of colors greeted the senses, one of the best-groomed golf courses I'd laid eyes on anywhere surrounded the manor house, with fairways, bunkers, and greens nestled into the rolling contours. The nearby lake was blanketed with black and white swans, there were deer grazing, and pink flamingos rounded out a scene of beauty and charm so intense that I couldn't resist the temptation to explore. With my camera and my faithful tools of trade—a shag bag full of balls—out onto the lawn I went.

I soon found a convenient practice tee and became engrossed in hitting balls when a most charming lady came strolling along.

"Do you mind if I watch you?" she asked. "I've been watching you from my window, and I've been having a problem with my golf game, a horrible slice. I thought perhaps I might learn something."

"Why, of course not," I replied.

As she settled onto the bank nearby, I asked her where she lived. She answered quite simply, "In London," and then asked me how long I was going to be staying.

"Oh," I said, "I'll be here for some time yet. Tell me about your slice. Have you been to any pros for advice?"

She assured me that she had and couldn't seem to correct it.

Looking down at her high-heeled shoes, I suggested, "You can't play in those high heels."

Almost shyly she took off her shoes, but hesitated to take a club.

"Go ahead and hit a few balls," I said. "Use any club you want."

She did, and she really had the biggest slice I ever saw, with the ball winging off to the right in a tight, fast loop.

"Well," I said, "it's quite obvious what's wrong. I see right away what your trouble is."

"What is it!" she almost pleaded.

"Why, my dear lady, you've got lazy hips!" I answered.

Looking at me a bit indignantly, she challenged, "Sir, and what's wrong with my hips?"

"Nothing wrong with your hips, lady," I hastily replied. "That's just an expression used in America when a person isn't pivoting, not turning properly, that's all."

Enjoying this, I went over and held her by the body and showed her what to do. She had never heard of pivoting and had been standing flat-footed, therefore, by necessity, slicing.

She immediately straightened out and hit some beautiful shots, even using my specially long clubs.

"Why, you're wonderful!" she said. "Nobody ever told me that before." And she inquired how she might have some further instruction. "Maybe in London?" she suggested.

There I was. I had been trying to find out her address and her telephone number, and she was going to help me. She was rather an attractive person, and I thought I was getting along all right. We bantered a bit more when she finally suggested, "I think you ought to come in for breakfast now. That hungry mob will have eaten up all the food."

She took me by the arm, leading the way through the pathways of the garden, and, just as we got to the house, I saw a tall stately gentleman coming toward us. I stopped in my tracks, stood there, and gasped, unable to speak, feeling plenty foolish. He extended his perfectly manicured hand as he approached and took mine in a warm grip. I recognized him immediately—King George VI!

Well, I was so mortified that I hadn't realized that I was with the queen that I fled to the cover of the golf course for the remainder of the day. Inevitably, though, three o'clock arrived, and I had to appear to do the exhibition. Still embarrassed that I hadn't shown the correct respect, words, and proper manners, I arrived at the last minute in front of a rather large audience of selected nobility. As I walked over to my big golf bag, everybody stood up. Thinking to myself, "That's funny; certainly the most wonderful reception I've ever received," my eye happened to travel back toward an opening in the aisle and there I saw the royal couple, the king and queen, walking toward me with the two young princes to take their places at the center chairs.

There were some 120 people present, kings and queens, lords and dukes, counts, and maybe a few no-accounts, who watched with rapt attention. When I was through, the queen, who didn't leave after the show with the others, came over to me.

"I owe you an apology." Her voice was full of warmth and gentleness. "It was a bit mean, not making myself known this morning. I wonder if you would have tea with me out on the patio?" Her eyes twinkled all the time she extended this kind invitation.

We crossed the lawn together again to the terrace, and

this lovely lady sat down beside me. She didn't say very much for a while, but her manner was kind. My discomfort started to fade, and I began to feel a bit less awkward. She asked me about my visit to her country and questioned me about the golf courses I'd played. She seemed sincere in her interest and listened intently to my replies.

Very quickly large trays of sandwiches of every variety were brought to our table. I felt overwhelmed by the whole experience and remarked, "This is a rather large tea, isn't it?"

"Oh!" she answered, "I'm afraid you haven't eaten anything today!"

I wondered how she had noticed my absence, but I was starved since I hadn't dared face anyone after my royal slip and had missed both breakfast and lunch.

When we finished our tea, she asked me to do another show for the house party they were having the next day and asked whether she might have some lessons following the exhibition.

This time when I answered, I addressed her as "Your Royal Highness," but instantly she raised her hand.

"Now," she said, a fleeting smile crossing her face, "Now you've spoiled everything!"

DEEP-DOWN DEVOTION

On my return to Australia, I received a rousing welcome. I'd done well by my country, with a second at Gleneagles, a good showing at the British Open, and a very important win at Lossiemouth, Scotland, where I led the field by thirteen strokes. All told, I had created quite a stir for my countrymen, and they were proud of their native boy.

Naturally, invitations were waiting for personal appearances, which pleased me tremendously. I'll never forget, however, that during the first exhibition at my home club in Sydney, just as I was doing a series of unusual shots hit with the wedge, a little girl of no more than ten ran out of the gallery and spread a dainty lace handkerchief on the ground. She stopped the play to pick up my divot gently, folding the four corners of her kerchief together, and then leisurely walked back into the crowd. All the time I just stood there dumbfounded while everyone else laughed. Eventually I continued with my show. The incident didn't stay with me in the rush of well-wishers following the exhibition, and I thought no more about it.

Seven or eight years later, after many miles of golf courses, tournaments, and exhibitions, I was visiting my homeland and Sydney again. (It was always one of my favorite stamping grounds.) Late in the afternoon of the first day I received a phone call at my hotel with the explanation that, although I didn't know the speaker, I had known her father. She made a very appealing request for me to stop and visit with her as she had "something to show me."

I did remember her dad as greens keeper, and so I decided to accept the invitation and made a date for a visit that next Sunday afternoon. Upon arriving, I couldn't help notice that it was a very modest and neat home, with flowers and careful plantings enclosed behind the typical black-iron-railing fence. The house itself lay back from the street and was perched on a hillside overlooking Manly Beach, the city, and the harbor. The young lady greeted me with an apology for having phoned; she was full of hesitation. She explained that there was something she had been saving, and I noticed her youth and radiance bubbling from within.

After discussing a variety of refreshments, we settled on tea and following this with some general chatter and reminiscences, she couldn't contain herself any longer.

"Come outside for your surprise, Joe. I think you'll be pleased."

Leading me first through to the porch, now made into a beautiful greenhouse filled with bowls of hanging rose blossoms, she continued outside to the lawn. Tilting her chin up, she nodded at the scene.

"There it is!"

I looked at her questioningly. "What do you mean?"

She laughed, but then replied very seriously. "There's your divot. I made it into a lawn for you!"

I stared at her unbelievingly. Over the years she had

17

tenderly nurtured that flying divot from my exhibition at the Manly Club and grown it into a complete lawn. There wasn't a weed or burnt patch in it. Each blade of grass stood straight as a brush bristle, and she had treated it all as hallowed ground. She had planted and separated, piece by piece, until she'd created a perfect yard as exquisite as a putting green. It was almost a monument of devotion.

She stood there, just a wee lass, slim and frail in an apple-green dress that set off her lovely complexion, clear blue eyes, and full inviting lips. There was something sweet, taunting, and yet impudent about the way she looked up at me to challenge, "Aren't you going to kiss me?"

I reached down for her without speaking and enfolded her in the most tender kiss of my life. The sensation of love that flooded through me was overwhelming. She was that little girl who had popped out of the crowd so many years ago to pick up my divot and had kept me in her heart for eight years. I felt suspended in space, flooded with emotion.

The afternoon waned rapidly. All too soon teatime had passed to dinnertime. The harbor started to glitter below with a myriad of lights. I have to admit that I left her reluctantly that evening, but through the following weeks I visited often. We walked the beaches together, talking about our futures. Her flattering need for me was one that I didn't want to destroy, and I almost fell completely in love. Inwardly, though, I knew that I was a born wanderer and could never stay, making our time together almost torture.

She touched me completely, and I knew that she would become a link of my life, one that I would return to, but one that I must leave now.

PART TWO

SOUTH AMERICA WITH SARAZEN

In 1933, the year I won the Canadian Open and Gene Sarazen won the PGA, we received an interesting offer to tour South America by Pan American clipper. In my travels to the golfing corners of the world, over eight thousand golf courses in all, I used every kind of transportation and mode of conveyance, but this inaugural trip by seaplane was one of the most exciting. They routed us down the east coast, stopping at Río de Janeiro, on to Montevideo and Buenos Aires, then crossing over the Andes to Chile, up the coast to Peru, and finishing in the West Indies.

Río, of course, is a most beautiful city, set dramatically with beach and mountainside so close by each other that it seemed impossible for there to be a golf course anywhere nearby. Upon our arrival, I decided to check on our exhibition arrangements, while Gene set out to see the sights. He didn't get very far because he discovered a swinging gambling room conveniently situated in our luxurious hotel. The Copacabana Beach was the top spot then, and Gene couldn't resist stepping inside for a moment's look at the action.

Several hours later he rushed back to our room, flung open the door, looked back out into the hallway, and quickly locked and double-bolted everything behind him. He even put a chair under the doorknob for a further brace against intruders. Then he raced over to the couch, tearing great wads of bills out of every pocket and corner of his jacket and trousers. He dug out thousands of reis and threw them down with near hysteria. He was absolutely wild with excitement and wanted to end the trip then and there, before it had hardly begun.

His manner so electrified me that I too grew excited. He explained that he had gone to the gambling casino downstairs and broken the bank.

"How much did you win?" I asked.

With which he replied in almost ecstasy, "I won three million!"

"Three million what?" I questioned.

"Three million of whatever money they have!" he shouted. "I've made it. No more traveling for me. Home we go. Count it if you like."

Well, it took me nearly an hour to sort it out. And there were some three million reis, all right. But when I'd finished (and by then he was a bit more calm), I thought aloud, "Gene, I hate to tell you this, but I just airmailed a letter back to the States, and it cost me sixteen thousand *reis* in stamps. I don't think you have quite enough to retire."

He stared at me with disbelief and asked just how much he had won in American dollars. I got out my pencil and paper and translated it to about $220.

"Aw, hell!" he said. "That's not enough. I'm taking it back down there to see if I can win some real money."

He stuffed the money back in his pockets and went muttering out the door. As expected, in a half hour or so he returned. He'd lost every *real*. His fortune had slipped away, but it didn't really solve anything anyway and seemed unreal, let alone countable. So there we were, partners and golfers again on tour, and it was up to me now to plan our schedule and make it pay. Following the matches in Río, we proceeded on to Buenos Aires. It was there that we played in a tournament against Pozi, the local Argentine hero.

A side bet of fifteen hundred dollars on the outcome made the game more juicy, and I'll never forget that tournament. The local women came out and knelt down right in the middle of the fairways, saying their rosaries and praying aloud for their favorites to win. Meanwhile, the men lined the back of the greens, and if the shot was over the mark, they stood firm and let the ball bounce off them like back-boards. A rather shady way to help their man, but somehow we came out the winners anyway.

Several days later we experienced the high point of the trip when we took a trip on one of the darnedest planes I've ever been on. The craft was a tin four-motor plane used for ferry service over the Andes. We hit some powerful down-drafts that day and simply didn't have the power to get over the peaks. We lacked several thousand feet in altitude, and although the pilot tried his best and paralleled the ridge of peaks, we couldn't get through. They call this area the Switzerland of South America, and the mountains rise over 21,000 feet. Crossing them was a tremendous task in those days, and there was no other choice but to return to Mendoza. The strong winds were doing a job on us, and we didn't even have oxygen on the plane. As a token, we each had a tube to a canister, and if we felt dizzy, we were supposed to inhale through the tube.

When he looked out the window and saw that we weren't going to make it, Sarazen dropped to his knees to say his

23

last prayers. I looked over at him saying, "We really are in some trouble, Gene, but what you're doing won't help a damn bit. We'll get out of this thing, just you watch."

Of course, by then we were in a slot between ridges and had dropped to the very bottom of a canyon. Eventually we turned and flew out with the wind behind us to help. Following our return to Mendoza for refueling, we made a fresh start, and this time we did make it. The whole voyage was designed for the fearless.

Later during the same trip we flew the length of the Andes with fog blanketing the scenery below us; just the mountain peaks alongside were visible. We flew up the coast of Chile to Antofagasta, where a military restriction forbade any commercial flights to fly closer to the coast than twenty miles. This put us right up against the rock faces, and Gene didn't like that either. It was quite a flight, but the pilot found a hole in the overcast and finally got us down beneath the billowing mists. We landed safely to make our schedule right on the button.

Actually, toward the end of this hitch, I found myself playing alone. Our passage north took in many of the smaller West Indian islands, and we stopped at places like Trinidad and Bridgetown in Barbados. Gene didn't want to play unless he was guaranteed a lump sum for the exhibition. I felt, however, that no matter how small and remote a group of golfers might be, they were still deserving; and if they were interested, I wanted to bring a bit of foolery and some good laughs into their lives. Sarazen and I had quite a number of disagreements on this subject. Most often I went off solo just to please the crowds, no matter what their size. I think I won a lot of friends for golf this way, and it was my own small contribution to life as it should be lived. But ultimately it was the reason for separating our partnership. When the

24

tour was over, we parted friends, but each of us went his own way with his own philosophy of life, and mine was that all golfers are brothers and that money was the least value of importance.

BUNKERED BY BABOONS

Going back again into partnership with Hagen seemed like a homecoming. Together we had eternal youth. One morning just after we'd finished an extensive European tour and were a bit golfed-out, we sat shooting the breeze, and I turned the conversation to travel.

"Haig, where would you like to go from here?"

"You're the boss," he answered. "Wherever you say."

With the straightest, most innocent face I could put on, I commented, "We've got quite a spell before our next match, several months to fool with. How about a trip to Africa?"

His reaction was instantaneous. The Haig was all for it.

This proposal called for a loan from me, since I was his ever-present business manager, banker, and soft touch. Off he went to the best sporting goods and safari equippers in London and picked out some of the fanciest and most expensive rifles, fishing gear, and camping paraphernalia that you've ever seen collected in one spot. He was busy for a day or two selecting the stuff—several thousand dollars' worth—and brought it back to me like a kid with a bag full of new toys.

My next task was to find a way to ship all these new purchases and us to the green continent below. I found that the most economical plan was to get a boat from Genoa, with overland transportation first to Marseilles and then to Italy. Arrangements made, on October 8, 1937, we embarked on the *Giulo Cesare* direct to Capetown. When we arrived, we booked some few incidental exhibitions to fill in our trip; in fact, wherever there was golf we put on the show, playing in some of the most remote places in the world where there weren't even courses. But strangely enough, enthusiasm and interest in the sport was generated by the few Europeans who lived there.

At dockside, upon arrival, we looked at our pile of luggage and decided that we needed some sort of conveyance—a pretty large one to house not only the golfing gear but also our hunting and camping equipment, maps, food, and the rest. We wanted something rugged that would take us through the jungle, yet something comfortable too.

Our first thought was to sound out the people at General Motors, but they didn't have anything. In discussing our plans, however, they told us that at Port Elizabeth where there had been a movie company on location, they thought there might still be a Land Rover–type house trailer left behind. The movie was finished, they believed, and perhaps the vehicle was still somewhere around.

With that valuable tip, we beat it down the coast and got hold of this marvelous car. It turned out to be four-wheel-drive, practical in every way. It had sleeping accommodations, a bar—just about everything. We felt that we had it made and started off with every confidence from New London north to Johannesburg. During our inquiries on the coast before departure, the authorities had advised us that there were two roads, both over rugged terrain. One road hadn't been used for at least six months, but it was miles and miles shorter than the roundabout, preferred route. By now Walter felt invincible in his new tanklike vehicle, and even though I felt some slight hesitation, I was game to try anything. Anyway, we decided to take the rough road.

The first sign of the true state of things came when we were faced with a number of washouts and deep ruts right at the start. As we dodged and detoured around rocks and rubble, we found ourselves stymied by fallen trees and logs and swollen creeks and streams. With such a beginning, I turned to Walter and asked, "What do you think, partner?"

He looked at me and answered, "You're the bushman from Australia, Kirkie. I have every confidence in you to get us through!" So on we pushed, and as we progressed I realized that we were traveling around the side of a high mountain. When we looked down, it was a drop of some thousands of feet to the river bed below, and though it had already been a pretty dangerous trip, we'd got so far in now that we couldn't turn around.

Midmorning we hit a huge, unexpected pocket hole in the road and with a resounding crack got our first flat tire. Both of us scrambled over the side to make repairs. Suddenly a big boulder came rolling down the hill toward us, directly toward the car. Walter turned to me, some of his gaiety gone, and questioned, "Hasn't been raining lately, Kirkie. Wonder what loosened that up?"

In no time other rocks came rolling down toward us, straight in our path as if we were a target. We couldn't move the darn vehicle—jacking it up was a task in itself. Thinking that this situation was sort of strange, I stopped for a moment and stood up to scan the side of the cliff to see if a crack or fault—perhaps an earthquake—was starting. Instead, high up on the edge of some woods I saw a troop of baboons, I'd say a hundred of them, deliberately pushing stones in our direction. Some of them had begun coming mighty close to the bull's-eye. What's more, as they exhausted their supply on the top level, they started moving in, closer and closer, getting braver and more brazen.

At this point I thought it best that I get to those lug nuts on the tire and get our car operational. Returning to the vehicle, I tore into the job. Grabbing a wrench, I spoke to Walter: "Well, Bwana, what are you going to do about this now? We're sort of getting attacked by the locals, you might say!"

Walter was grinning all over. He just straightened up from the tire tools and said, "Kirkie, you take care of the details. I think I'll just have to try out those new rifles!"

Somehow, though, I had a tighter feeling about this bombardment than he, and I countered: "Listen, the car will wait. I think I'll load the rifles for you and get into this thing myself."

By this time we realized that only the males were coming in close, while the females and young kept to the high ground. Some of the males were very persistent and advanced as near as twenty to thirty yards from us. Grabbing our guns, we started popping them off, one by one, but the animals seemed inexhaustible and very plentiful. In fact, the parched clay was turning color with the bodies littered about, and our rifles were heating up with the unnatural number of consecutive rounds of firing. Hagen, by the way, proved to be an unusual marksman with these new guns. We used not only the untested rifles but our 12-gauge shotguns too.

I must admit that we were both scared, it being our first encounter in the interior of Africa. However, quite suddenly without any real reason, these fellows set up a terrific hollering, a sort of screeching and calling, and as if at some secret signal they took off. It was totally amazing to us. Walter, of course, was enjoying the whole thing, but I had no interest in killing anything and had brought only a camera as weapon for my "shooting safari." But there we were, hardly begun and almost bunkered by baboons—an eerie start to our adventures. After the animals had departed and our car was repaired, we somehow found our way out and away from that awful road. Every other trail seemed easy after this baptism, and following this episode we agreed to stick to the better-traveled paths.

MATCH FOR THE PREACHER

Several days passed, and then we arrived at a small junction of roads, still very near the jungle. We stopped for petrol, and Walter got into a conversation with the owner of the gas station and asked if there were any towns nearby and, jokingly, if there were any with a golf course. To our complete surprise, we were told there was a town "with some links" not more than a mile or two away. With a mutual nod we decided to investigate and rolled in, really looking a sorry lot. It was a tossup which looked worse for wear, us or our trailer van. In no time, however, we found the sheriff's office and inquired whether any lodging was available—we wanted to soak off the jungle dirt. Fortunately, we hit it right on the nose; the local constable had rooms and seemed glad to have us join him. We told him we were traveling through Africa on a hunting trip and thought we'd take a small detour and stop there for a visit.

Following a quick clean-up, Walter wandered downtown to the local saloon to "sort of get the flavor of the place." Meanwhile, I did some unpacking and settling in. Soon enough Hagen had a new set of buddies. He later said that the talk mostly consisted of hunting stories—tales of various animals and where to find them. After several hours I joined him, thinking a sandwich might be in order. I was never a drinker or smoker, which was just as well, because someone had to keep his wits about him, and that task continued to be mine. Afternoon turned into evening. The pace of life in such towns as this was rather lazy, and around about dusk the local preacher turned up at the bar. He had got word that a titled Englishman had just arrived in town—"Sir Walter," who was ensconced in the saloon spending money like a drunken sailor. I imagine this man of God figured that if the new arrival was buying everybody drinks he might get a small handout for his cause.

Well, Hagen thought the new arrival seemed a fine fellow and tried to get him a few donations, but meanwhile he found that the preacher hadn't been doing well financially. He'd been pastor in the community for twenty years, but was short of cash. Walter immediately decided to take up a collection. With his usual style, he bought drinks for all and rose to his feet, saying to the assembled patrons: "Look, I'm afraid we haven't done right by this good man sitting here. He tells me you haven't been inside his chapel for ages. I'd like to contribute something towards his welfare, so if you'll unzip your pockets, anything that you give, I'll double." Turning to me on the quiet, he mumbled, "Kirkie, give me ten pounds."

At that time ten pounds sterling was equivalent to fifty dollars, and that started it off. The end result was seventy pounds collected, which Walter then doubled, giving the churchman quite a boost. The old preacher was so thrilled that his joy and pleasure brought tears to his eyes. Walter, then, to top things off, ordered champagne for everybody, and the preacher, who at first was reluctant to join in, decided it only right to have "just one" to show his appreciation.

After quite a while, at everybody's urging, he had another. This led, of course to another, and so on all evening, the preacher protesting and Walter urging him on "to celebrate the wonderful support of the people for the Church"—surely reason to rejoice. Well, this happy wet scene flowed on and on. Suddenly I noticed a lady standing at the door of the bar. The man next to me identified her as the preacher's wife. I crossed the room to explain to her what had happened—the collection, her husband's happiness, the small celebration. She was most astounded with it all, exclaiming that her husband had never touched a drop of spirits in his life and that she felt some concern for him. I assured her that everything was fine and that I would personally guarantee her husband's well-being. I also volunteered to see her home, since it was some distance to their house along the village path. However, she refused, saying that her only worry was for her husband.

By now Hagen had got the preacher quite tight. His steady sipping made it impossible for him even to stand, let alone walk. Although his wife left him in my care, she returned quietly to look in on him on three different occasions that evening. At closing time we all agreed that it was necessary to go somewhere, but before leaving, Hagen got one last bottle of wine and managed to slip it into the preacher's pocket. Arm in arm they weaved out to the bit of pavement in front of the bar, where, unfortunately, the preacher slipped and fell, breaking the bottle. The contents spilled to the ground, and the fragrance saturated the air. Hagen then decided that he would have to walk the good man home because he'd "spoiled his clothes."

Up the path to the preacher's house they went, singing, and apologizing to each other. When they arrived at the top of the hill, the preacher turned to Hagen and exclaimed, "You don't know the way back!" And he insisted on escorting his visitor home! Down they went, happily cementing their friendship, helping each other. This went on for three trips—Hagen accompanying the preacher up, the preacher leading the way down, Hagen all the while teaching the preacher dirty ditties, broadening his outlook. When dawn came, they somehow parted.

The next day in the hotel lounge, the preacher confided to Walter that he had done all right in the town until they built the nine-hole golf course. But now, instead of coming to church, his congregation was always at the course, and his services were unattended. As the conversation progressed, several people gathered around, and they turned to Walter, asking whether he'd ever tried the game of golf.

"Oh," he answered, "I've played a little, but I'm not here to chase the ball, just some of those game animals you have out there in the bush." Hagen then asked them the number of golfers they had and if they were any good. By now, on safer ground, they answered that there were about twenty-seven members and some "quite talented."

"Tell you what I'll do, gents. My man Kirkie and I will play the whole club," said Walter. "We'll take on the pack—your best ball against us."

Naturally, they thought that this newcomer was just sounding off, that he had more money than sense. However, being the good Scotsmen they were, none could resist a bet. The talk swung with odds and numbers, and it was decided that I should handle the money, the local constable keeping the tally.

At this point I was a bit curious to find out whether any of these blokes recognized us. To put my mind at ease, I began asking around the group if they had ever heard of Bobby Jones.

"No," they said.

"Or Sarazen?"

"No."

It became obvious that they also weren't familiar with the reputation of the English players either. In fact, this parting in the bush was so remote that they hardly recognized the names of the international golfing "greats." So a match was set for the following Saturday with the entire membership pitted against us two.

On the next day, while Walter organized some hunting, I decided to take a trip out to the course to have a look around. I didn't put on my golfing gear but kept my bush clothes on and took along a couple of old clubs. I found things very primitive. They had just carved this place out of the bush, and Tanganyika didn't have the most ideal vegetation for golf. They were pretty proud of their links though, and rightly so. I learned that when the club was first founded the twenty-seven members split up into teams of three and each built a hole, doing all the work themselves. When I looked at the scorecard, I noted the strange names they had given to the various holes: "It Is," "Jocks Jungle," "Hit It," "Hookers Home," "Leopard Lake," "Top Hole," and "At Last." As at Gleneagles and other courses in the Old Country, particularly Scotland, they had given a name instead of a number to each hole. A fine old custom, I thought. The clubhouse, too, was home-grown, with an attractive thatched roof built of sturdy bamboo with bougainvillaea blooms covering practically every part of it—a beautiful sight.

Upon my arrival I noticed a few members gathered in the

shade, quietly watching my every move. With this surveillance, I didn't feel that I could do any real practicing and decided to play the duffer and miss my shots. I did a good job of it, with hooks, slices, and shanks, and somehow managed to lose all my balls in the jungle. That night it became obvious that the word had got out about my practice session; everybody wanted to raise his bet. It seemed that the whole town became part of it; everyone wanted a piece of the action. The wager price leveled at seven to two, all of which I hesitantly covered.

When Walter learned what I'd done, he howled, and with his best British accent said, "Good show, old boy, jolly good!"

Luckily our assets at that time were good; we were solvent, with a balance to boot. We had amassed a sizable chunk of money from the recent five months' tour of England and the Continent and could meet the bets on the match, which had now risen to alarming proportions. In fact, word had spread to several other small, relatively faraway communities. It was to be a gala event, so much so that the merchants decided to declare a public holiday. The general store, trading post, and all places of business, including the only beer joint, were to be closed.

When Saturday arrived, I went out to the club early. Hagen was to follow. Preceding his arrival, though, he sent kegs of beer and bottles of liquor and wine, all to be set out in tubs under the trees. He did this as a good-will gesture and, of course, hoped that the membership would get a bit tight too, with the sun and heat as his allies. His strategy worked. They all dipped in and enjoyed Walter's hospitality while he kept them waiting. After about an hour I became a little worried and set out to find him. The Haig never hit any practice balls; his theory was that he only had so many shots in his bag, so why waste any? I had no sooner started back toward town when I found him, in a clearing off the dirt road, teaching a bunch of fifteen- and sixteen-year-old native girls to do the shimmy! What a sight their brown bodies were, all youth and jiggle, alive with rhythm, and only their beads for cover.

Somehow I tore him away, and we headed to the course for the match. By this time I was genuinely worried about our wager. By now there were thousands of dollars riding on the outcome, and I told Hagen that eventually these people were bound to find out who we were, and they would think us a pair of bandits.

"Heck, no, Kirkie," he said. "The whole idea was theirs. They thought we were just two soft suckers. But I'll give them a chance to call off their bets if you want."

When we arrived, Walter made an announcement. "Look," he said, "we didn't come here to play a golf match but to hunt. And you people have got in sort of deep on this betting deal. You've all been so friendly to me and my pal, we'd just as soon play for fun. I want to give you the opportunity to call it off. Anybody who wants to change his mind go to my man here. Kirkie will take your name, and we'll forget the whole thing."

Unbelievably, there was only one person who stepped up to me with a change of heart, the constable. With his name recorded, Walter turned to me and said, "Let's get on with the match, old buddie. Show me where to go."

The Haig and I played that day in our khaki hunting outfits. We had decided it wasn't wise to dress and look too much the part of golfers. All the others, though, had on their golfing plus fours and brightly polished shoes and sported their new clubs. We had only our small canvas golf bags, which we used when girl caddies were available (as is the custom in many foreign countries). We looked pretty insignificant in contrast to our opposition.

On the first tee Walter suggested tossing a coin to decide which side would have the honor, but their captain insisted that "visitors always hit first." So Walter motioned to me to lead the way. Without so much as a forward glance, I stepped up and sliced a big wild one, looping over the jungle but back onto the fairway at the finish. I turned to Hagen when it landed and remarked, "Gosh, that's a new one. I've never done that before!"

Walter countered, "That's the bad grip that pro down in Durban showed you. You're bound to slice now."

All the while we noted that my ball was in a good position, well down the fairway, short of a lagoon with the green just beyond. Since I was sitting there for an easy pitch shot, Walter grabbed his driver and hit a tremendous wham, sending it right down the alley and onto the green; the ball even rolled beyond the flag. Nobody had ever tried for the pin on his drive; it was just too far out and involved accurate placement as well. Ordinarily Walter wasn't an exceptionally long hitter, but when it was necessary he had the jolt of a giant. This one golf shot completely cooled the confidence of the local lads. One drive doesn't usually decide the fate of a golf match, but that colossal one surely did, and the whole gallery groaned with amazement.

The second hole was a par three, about 185 yards, with hard ground in front of the tee. I took a four wood and half-topped the ball; it bounded down the hill like a jackrabbit from Wyoming, finally finishing on the front side of the green. On my third tee shot, I skied high, and the ball ended burrowed deep into the fairway. Walter leaned toward me and quipped, "Well, it was straight anyway! But don't let it bother you, Kirkie. You'll adjust your stance after a while.

Meantime, I hope we don't run out of holes. I'll see if I can help you after this shot."

Following that, on every hole during the long wait for the others to hit, Walter would take me aside and change my grip, stance, or something in my swing. Desperately the local players tried their utmost to make a game of it, but their knickers and spirits showed signs of sagging. In fact, it took quite a time for the local line-up to get underway. Most of their shots strayed deep in the brush, and few finished out the holes. Loss of all their balls sent some to the sidelines; others were so tense and nervous that they even had trouble teeing up.

When we reached the fifth green, a tropical broccoli putting surface was waiting. Walter winked at me, saying, "Watch this, Kirkie. I've got a sinking feeling." And sink it he did, drilling the eagle putt straight for the cup.

As far as the outcome of the match was concerned, it turned out to be a blitz, never in doubt. A spectator asked my caddie how the game was going: "How many holes up are you?"

The lass answered, "We is all up!"

About that time, when the results were secure, both Walter and I purposely dubbed a few shots and let the opponents win the last two holes. It eased their sorrow a bit. But we had fared far better than I thought we would. I figured at least one of the opponents would be in there with a par or better on each hole. But apparently the pressure of money was too great, and it didn't work out that way.

The next morning we decided that it was best to leave, quickly and quietly. The preacher insisted that we were to have breakfast with him, and I hustled with the packing. I had put all the winnings into a shoebox and then transferred the box to the bottom of my large golf bag. All stowed, we started up to the preacher's house along the road that led both to the golf course and to the church. When we reached the club sign, I had an idea and stopped the car. At the junction of the road that led to the church I got out and tied the sign to a tree, pointing the words "To the Golf Club" right toward the chapel.

Following a delightful breakfast we bade our farewells to the preacher, thanking him and his kind wife for their hospitality. They urged us to stay for the service, but we declined. We said that we had a small offering which we wanted to leave with them. I excused myself for a moment and went out to get our shoeboxful of winnings. Those several thousands of dollars were very heavy, and I placed them on the table saying, "Preacher, this is our contribution to your service. Please don't open it until after the collection is taken."

With no further words we left, feeling good in our hearts. There are certain things in life you can't buy. Peace and contentment rate high on that list, and beauty must be lived. Throughout that humble home it certainly was.

STYMIED BY LIONS

Heading east, we decided on a circular route across to Zanzibar, the exotic island on the Azanian Sea, which meant a trek through most of Tanganyika. It took us five full days of hard driving through wild country, but we pointed toward the coast since we eventually planned to go south for an exhibition at the Kimberley diamond mines.

I think that the company course of that South African business was one of the most memorable I've ever played. Instead of normal greens, these people had replaced conventional grass with chips of amethysts and other soft gems. When the sun hit this surface, the "greens" glowed with a pink, radiant fire. It made you want to bend down and scoop up a handful to take with you. Truly a fantastic experience, and though the gem dust had no great commercial value, it sparkled and glistened, catching the sun in a rainbow of prisms.

To recap just a bit, however, after we left the preacher, we traveled down from the Mountains of the Moon past melting snows that, joining, surged down through Lake George

41

and Lake Edward to meet the Victoria Nile. This water body spills from Lake Victoria and eventually floods the deserts of the Sudan on the way to Egypt. We drove first through Uganda, which runs generally on a high plateau about 4,000 feet above sea level. The scenery here was as green and gentle as Ireland in the sunshine. Next we climbed to the Gishu plateau and skirted Mount Elgon, a 14,178-foot extinct volcano. When we crossed the equator, we were at an altitude of 9,136 feet; then we dropped down to Kenya through the Rift Valley. Truly the contrasts of these short days of spectacular mountains, windswept plains, and plunging cataracts, all brilliant with sunlight, made our senses alert and flooded us with a feeling of wonder.

The game in Kenya was supposed to be the most plentiful in all of Africa, and Hagen was itching for some serious hunting. We agreed to keep our eyes ready for a good camping site, and about the end of the third day we were really getting to the heart of the safari country. We had come across some heavily grassed plains to a crevasse with a river running deep through its center and decided to parallel its course to watch for a good crossing. The first obstacle we noticed was a group of hippos bathing, and we gave them a wide berth. Driving on, feeling more dusty and thirsty by the minute, we couldn't resist the water and decided on a swim. We parked our conveyance as near the water as possible, but there was a steep bank to negotiate, and we had no choice but to leave our car on top.

In a matter of minutes we piled out of that van and slid down the bank into the fast ripple. It felt great on our naked white bodies, and we started to soap up for a good swim. We edged out toward the middle, and I to the deeper water where I lazily turned over to watch the sun start down behind the scrub trees. Instead of seeing a purple-and-orange spectacle, my eyes somehow stopped at the bank, where they became fastened on a whole family of lions—seven of them! They had quietly arrived as we were wading out midstream and were positioned between us and our car. Undoubtedly they had come to take their evening wash too. But what company! I can only describe our reaction by saying that the water definitely wasn't fit to drink any more.

With rising feelings of discomfort mixed with more than faint fear, we stood neck-deep in the river for what seemed an eternity. Those beasts of the jungle kept us trapped there for more than three hours. The bad part of the scene was that Walter couldn't swim. I searched my mind for some way to get us out of this jam, but we were at a standoff. The lions didn't know quite what we were, Hagen couldn't get into the deep water, and we weren't able to get back to our car for rifles or clothes!

As a rule lions do their killing in the evening. It was obvious that they were waiting for us to get out of there, and yet I thought that we were better off staying in the water, hoping eventually they would get tired and leave. Meanwhile, I also decided that we had better have some protection should they try to make a move toward us. But what could we use? I looked across the river, which was pretty wide at this point, with a good current in the center of its bed. On the other side were quite a number of saplings growing at the water's edge. Telling Walter to stay where he was, I decided to swim over and take a look. As I'd hoped, the young trees pulled up pretty easily. I grabbed the two largest ones that I could find, leaving the roots on them, and stripped off the branches so that with their stumps they measured about six to eight feet.

I ferried the first one back to Hagen, saying, "Here, Haig, practice your swing. You haven't had a club in your hands

43

for quite a few days!" Then I swam back to the other side to retrieve the remaining one for myself. With this small improvement in equipment, we felt a little better about our situation. Luckily the water was warm, but after a few hours we were really becoming saturated.

By now I had thought of trying to swim up- or downstream and circle around to get to our car, but every time I would move off, the mother lion would follow my path and pace the bank, which neutralized my progress. The evening deepened into semidarkness, while the slow lashing of the big animals' tails and the occasional snarling of the female to her cubs entertained us. With the light almost gone, Walter and I decided that perhaps our only move was to advance forward, swinging the tree clubs in front of us like shillelaghs. At an agreed signal we started making a terrible commotion in the water, slapping it with all our strength to make the loudest racket possible. Incredibly, the male stood up and stretched his whole body out toward us. Hagen followed with some more wild splashing maneuvers, and I hit some of the longest "back swings" with the best "follow throughs" of my career. Unbelievably that did it. Suddenly the whole family got up and retreated off the bank and went away.

You've never seen two fellows get out of the tub faster. We made a dash for our car, with Hagen swearing that he was going to get that male if his life depended on it! Once in our van we moved along the river for a very short spell, while I was driving and Walter was reaching for his bottle of something other than water, but we really were pretty exhausted and decided to call it a day.

The next morning we were sure that that same family of beasts was close by. Then we noticed some vultures circling above, a sure sign of a kill, for the big birds follow to devour the leavings. Just beyond our grove of trees we came upon the remains of a hartebeest. Walter caught sight of his prey. He delightedly bagged the big boy as his trophy. As for me, I credited golf with saving a serious situation for us both.

WIVES GALORE

Our trip progressed much in this pattern—golf exhibitions, hunting, rolling with the punches—but before leaving that interesting continent, there was one place we just had to check out. We had heard numerous tales about the natives and their way of life and, in particular, a story about one tribal chief.

Hagen had got wind of a rumor that there was a Zulu king who had 103 wives. The Haig became intrigued with this accomplishment and insisted that we make a detour to Bulawayo to find this king and learn his secrets. Before leaving Mombassa, we had stocked our van with some choice liquor (to keep the snakes away), and I had laid in a supply of colored beads that I carried along for emergencies. I had learned from others that there was nothing that would please the natives more than these bright ornaments—they adorned themselves with the things—and it was a quick and easy method of making friends. In fact, they accepted the gaudy, cheap trinkets with overwhelming delight, enjoying the color and light of them. Perhaps they thought them priceless jewels.

For days and many miles we skirted the lowlands and swamps that lay around the great lake region. Word of mouth helped us, and we had no trouble finding the chieftain once we set out in earnest. To our amazement we found that he did indeed have just that many wives, more than one hundred of them, and each one had a hut and family of her own. The chief himself was wealthy not only by measure of wives, but also in cattle and land. He had fruit trees and simple crops and was well organized in every way. Upon our arrival the old fellow welcomed us and showed us about. Walter, ever the enthusiastic hunter, expressed a wish to do some small gaming, and over some friendly refreshment we started up a conversation. Actually Walter did want to hunt some more, but, more important than that, he wanted to find out what this giant ate in order for him to be able to keep all of those wives happy. He was more than curious about the chief's sex life—one man and all those women.

He found out after discreet inquiry that the secret to the man's prowess was due to a diet of baboon meat and rhino horn. At that time it was believed all through Africa and India that ground-up horn powder was an aphrodisiac. Baboon meat was also supposed to stimulate and increase man's reproductive power tremendously. When Walter heard that, he said, "That's for me!" and immediately became sold on the idea. In fact, he ate that miserable fare at almost every meal. I was expecting to see him climbing the trees at any moment, he fell so completely into the spirit of the experiment.

Meanwhile, I couldn't help but admire this most attractive setting. Each of the women had her own house, surrounded by shrubs and flowers. The children seemed to appear from every corner, creating a happy, healthy atmosphere. And, idyllically, running right through the grounds there was a mountain stream and waterfall that attracted the mothers for their washing and the children for play.

All activity centered about the chief's hut, and after our week's stay we had become good friends. I admired some interesting carvings on his walls, and at our departure he insisted that we take them with us. Meanwhile, Walter with his diet of baboon steaks was having some uncomfortable consequences. The only real effect he realized was a high degree of constipation, but he couldn't be persuaded. He was so determined to abide by his new-found discovery that in the end I had to find him a doctor! That was what finally forced us back to civilization. Walter was prescribed the largest pills ever taken by man (they looked better suited for a bull elephant than human beings). So out of the bush we reluctantly came, many adventures wiser, with memories to match those "wives galore!"

PART THREE

SLIGHTLY SLIGHTED

Back in the early 1920's, after my first tournaments, I promised my friends and golfing fans down under that I would bring the great Walter Hagen to tour our country. However, it wasn't until 1936 that I persuaded the Haig to take a world trip with me, and our first stop was Australia. We had a series of exhibitions all over the country, including one in Canberra, the capital.

I was showing Walter my homeland with vast pride, pointing up things of interest, taking him to all the very fine Australian golf courses, and highlighting the great sights and scenes throughout the land. At that time the prime minister was James H. Scullin, and owing to his kindness we were to be given a royal welcome when we reached Canberra. Walter, being more or less an ambassador of his country because of his fame in the golfing world, took on a new dimension.

On the day before our arrival in the capital we had been playing Melbourne, and that night we left by sleeper train for the trip north. When we reached the borderline of the states of Victoria and New South Wales, there was a crazy arrangement in which we changed trains at Aubury to switch onto a narrow-gauge track. This transfer came in the middle of the night, of course, and took some time. At the stopover, Walter became friendly with some people on the train and proceeded to have quite a wet whirl of a party. By the time it had ended and he saw the beginnings of the new dawn, the train was well on its way to our destination, scheduled to arrive by nine in the morning.

He knew that we were going to be greeted by officials, the prime minister, Billie Hughes, and members of the Australian Parliament. Representatives of the press, radio, and the golf association would all be there. The red carpet was really out for him. Naturally, Walter had his own compartment, and just before arrival time I went to waken him, but he wouldn't open the door. He was stubborn as a mule could be and didn't answer my calls. He had bolted the entry from the inside and was feeling secure as a kitten from the world. He was snoring up a real storm.

Meanwhile, I was becoming frantic with all those dignitaries waiting for his appearance. The band played, young girls in short skirts were twirling batons, and I kept pounding at the door, calling, "Come on, Walter, they're all out there waiting for you."

Midst all this ruckus he yawningly turned over and mumbled, "It's the middle of the night, Kirkie, go away and let me sleep. Tell them I'll meet them for lunch."

This touch of diplomacy was way off wicket, putting me in the middle. Being an Australian by birth, I felt responsible for the whole production, and there seemed no doubt that I would have to abandon all hope of getting my bedswaddled partner up. In anguish I searched my mind for an adequate excuse. Finally I gathered up the courage to go out to the assemblage and explain, "Look, I've been down to his room and he ate something last night that didn't agree with him. He's got a bad case of ptomaine poisoning. You'd better send for a doctor, and he probably needs some rest."

While I was agonizing about what to do next, the thought suddenly occurred to me that an old friend of mine—and a golfer too—was the local undertaker. Instead of sending for the doctor, I sent a message for the undertaker to call on Walter. When he arrived, we both heavy-fisted that door, but there was still no reply, and I set out to find the station master. Luckily, the man just happened to have a set of extra keys for all the trains, which was a miracle because those compartments are tight and impenetrable and the Haig might have embalmed himself right there.

At last the undertaker knocked at the door and slowly opened it with the master key. Hagen rolled over and grouchily snapped, "What do you want?"

In surprise the coroner looked at me and answered, "There's supposed to be a dead man here."

Walter chirped up, "Dead to the world you mean. It's too early. I've never been late this early before!"

By this time it was well into the middle of the morning, and the situation wasn't improving one bit. Finally I came up with an idea. Leaving the Haig to his shiggered slumber, I hopped a cab out to the golf club and confided the seriousness of my dilemma to the pro. I asked him if there were any good-looking gals around, and three lovely young things were soon found.

We arrived back at the station complete with the girls, who were convulsed in giggles. As we boarded the traincar, their sweet-sounding voices outside the compartment door soon had Walter's corpuscles jumping. They succeeded in awakening him from his sleep all right, but found him still in his knickers and full golf attire. However, they did their wooing well, and he finally rose and dressed for that luncheon.

By this time the railroad people had moved the car well back into the yard, and we were a good distance from the platform and other transportation. All of which meant that I had a vigorous hike with all the suitcases and equipment to get out of the train single-handed. It was a good mile up the tracks for me, and while the girls took Walter to the club, I went downtown with all our gear and checked on our accommodations.

A half hour later, arriving at the club, I found Hagen on the practice tee near the putting green talking to a large group of people. Seeing me, he stopped his socializing, turned, and said, "Kirkie, where the hell have you been? We've been waiting here all morning for you!"

The ever-lighthearted Haig had done it again, laughed and lucked his way out of a delicate diplomatic situation. Face was saved for America and Australia all the way around, but it was an unplayable lie to be sure.

PYTHON PLAYMATE

During our travels the Haig and I had a date to play an exhibition in Singapore. It was a rule of Hagen's never to practice before a match. Therefore, I was alone that day. Leaving Walter to wander through the incredible array of shops and narrow thoroughfares, I headed out to the golf club to take a look around, refresh my memory of the course, and make the last-minute arrangements for the show.

The pro there was most cordial and persuaded me to play a few holes, rounding up two other members. We set forth in good style, and I was immediately attracted to the lushness of the surroundings. The course was half links, following the natural contours of the land and some manmade fairways planted with exotic flowering trees. After the first few holes, we came to an obvious blind dogleg. I wasn't quite sure of it and asked the way to the green. Pointing out across a large gully, the others suggested, "Right over there."

I took out my driver and played the shot, but it landed in the ravine. As I looked over the edge, my eyes threaded past the undergrowth of jungle, where I saw a python, thirty-

55

four feet long, with my ball right up against him! It was just a joke on their part, but they tried to inveigle me down there. Well, I wouldn't go and just shook my head at the suggestion that this monster wouldn't do anything danger-ous—maybe just wrap around me. The more they talked about retrieving that ball, the more I smiled, but without argument finished up the hole and continued with the match. A most enjoyable round among men of my kind and liking, full of camaraderie.

The next day was the scheduled exhibition. After a good start Hagen reached this same spot and, turning to me, he asked, "Where do we go here, Kirkie?"

"Oh, right across there," I waved.

And he hit the ball out just as I had, down into the gully and straight to the python who had just swallowed a whole pig! You could see the big outline bulging in him as the beast lazily swallowed and moved his huge head.

Walter took one look, and the exhibition stopped. There was nothing he wanted better than that python. He just had to catch it, crate it, and send it home to America. I knew he had a passion for animals, remembering the time in Aus-tralia when he wanted to send a kangaroo back to his boy in Detroit and another incident in India when the maharaja, who was a prince, gave him a little baby elephant in ap-preciation for our show. (He wanted to ship that back too, but I stopped him by pricing the freightage, which came to some $5,000, and Hagen settled for a girl out of the harem instead.) But there was no denying the fact that Walter had a real affection and love of animals and was determined to have this python from Singapore for his own.

However, for that moment I prevailed upon him to leave it behind and move along. Naturally, he played his ball from the ravine anyway. His shot was a good one, too, and the gallery was pleased as punch. Funny thing. Finishing up we learned that Frank Buck, the famous game hunter, was in town at the time and was staying at the same hotel we were, the Raffles. Our suite of rooms on the ground floor overlooked a beautiful garden with flowers in full bloom and lawns manicured to the last blade. Before I knew it, the Haig had made contact with Frank and arranged to have him send out some men to capture the python. In fact, it was delivered that same day.

"Well, now," I said, "what are you going to do with it? We're going to be here for three weeks at least, and it's going to cost too much to ship it back to the States. Where will we even put the thing?"

Since this was just the first of many dates we had to play in the Malaysian States, in Kuala Lumpur, Jahore and other places, I had visions of the snake as our constant companion. But nothing would hold Walter back. We got an extra room so that he could bring the python into the hotel—a connecting room—and he put the beast into the bathtub, into a gleaming white tub, enameled, with high sides that rested on feet that looked like giant paws. And the snake curled up in the tub, filling it completely. Walter named him Singo.

Naturally the next thing Walter wanted to know was what to feed his python. Buck counseled that the food which pleased the snake's appetite the most was raw eggs, four dozen of them a day. So the snake became ensconced in our bathroom opposite the living room, crushing and eating eggs!

During the following day, while we were still playing our exhibition, there was a particular girl in the gallery who caught our attention. Inspired by her, Walter decided that it was an appropriate time to have a party, and so he invited some twenty people down to our rooms that evening, among them the charming young lady. She was one of the most prominent debutantes of Singapore—young, pretty, with a striking figure, but timid, not sophisticated. True to form, anything could happen when I was traveling with Walter. He never failed to find fun, and ways and means to keep the days dancing along at a merry pace. And so the guests started arriving, the cocktails pouring, and the Haig turning on the charm. His good looks, suave manner, and dress captivated his new friends as always, and his attentions to this particular young lady were polite, almost gallant.

Presently our miss, upon whom all the attention was being focused, excused herself and headed toward the bathroom. Before I could stop her, she had slipped behind the door and quietly closed it. I looked over to Walter in horror. He whispered back, "Aw, it's okay. I pulled the shower curtain around Singo. She'll be all right—never even notice!"

The first instant was quiet, but then the most blood-curdling, piercing shriek came from behind that door. Apparently the python, content with its secluded surroundings, was disturbed when the young lady settled onto the seat, and he decided to investigate the rude intrusion by putting his head through the opening of the shower curtain. In a state of frenzy, the panic-stricken lady leaped down from the seat, bolted from the bath, stumbling out with her pink unmentionables hobbling her dainty ankles. As she burst through the door screaming, the scene was so hilarious that the guests, at first surprised, broke into wild spasms of laughter, further adding to her humiliation.

At that moment it was far from funny to her. In fact, I found her outside in quite a state of fright. I believe I was the only person present who realized this, and although I tried to soothe her, there was no way of explaining or getting her to return to the party. Instead, she insisted on a cab, and I escorted her home, apologizing all the way.

By the time I returned, the party had all but ended. Furiously I confronted Walter.

"You barnacle-brained numbskull," I raved, "you almost scared that poor girl to death. She's in a state of shock." And she was.

Several days later, I noticed that the snake had begun to smell. The odor was tremendous, and I said to Walter: "You've got to get this thing out of here. We can't keep it any longer. The manager is bound to get wind of it. The maids have to clean, and they won't go in there. Let's get rid of the reptile."

Walter would buy none of it, insisting it was a harmless pet. The more stubbornly he insisted on keeping his mascot, the more I became determined to be rid of him. On the following day we had a break from the tour, and Walter decided to go into town for a shopping spree and also to try to reach his lady friend, by phone or otherwise. I decided to stay behind at the hotel and make some "future arrangements." These arrangements included opening our bathroom window and carefully placing some eggs on the sill to entice our friend into moving. Sure enough, after a short wait, I heard a stirring and slithering, and the next thing I knew, Singo had left the tub, gone up onto the window casing and finally out and on his way. The last I saw of him he was weaving through the flower beds, destroying everything in his path for yards, heading toward a giant bougainvillaea vine, acting like a steam roller on the way over a cliff.

Where he finally finished nobody knew or cared—only Walter, who hoped he would return to his home in the gully on the golf course whence he came.

SULTANA

While Walter was concentrating on his python playmate, my spare time in Singapore was taken up in another department. During one of the many dinners to which we were kindly invited by local socialites, I found myself seated next to a dinner companion of exceptional charm and beauty. There was no doubt that this young woman was the center of all eyes, stunningly lovely and completely different from any other woman I had ever met.

The way golf cuts across the lives and social strata of all those whom I met never failed to amaze and intrigue me. Although at this time I was being wooed by the prominent, the next occasion might involve an out-of-the-way native host of the islands or a business tycoon or even royalty. One thing that always impressed me in my travels and lured me on was the variety and spice of life and how golf encompasses participants in untold occupations and of manifold interests.

There I was at the Raffles Hotel, surrounded by Victorian luxury and seated next to a petite miss who seemed not only mysterious but so demure and gentle that I couldn't believe that she came from any generation, west or east. With every male head turned her way, she seemed rapt in our conversation. She didn't listen like a bored sponge but made intelligent comments that showed she was paying attention to what I was saying. She seemed devoid of vanity and oblivious of anyone else at our party. At the end of our first evening together, I tried in my bumbling Australian way to find out her name and see whether I could get in touch with her again. But she totally escaped me. Not only did she not disclose who she was but in the confusion of saying good night to the hosts, she slipped away to her own car and a waiting chauffeur.

It wasn't long, however, before I ran into her again. At the very next social engagement, whom should I see seated neatly in one of the huge rattan chairs but my tiny new friend. She smiled warmly at me with her dark-brown eyes, growing larger in the evening twilight. I was completely smitten. In fact, I rather rudely ignored the other guests in my pursuit of this special one, and as the party progressed, I managed to learn that she lived some distance from the city. She explained that the reason for her car and driver was that it would be too far to impose on a stranger to return her home. In the end I won out. I dismissed her chauffeur, promising her that I would consider it a personal favor if she would let me escort her wherever she wished to go.

That time of the year was the start of the monsoon season, and the tropical storms often halted my demonstrations. So my schedule was rather a loose one, and I had time on my hands. Well, one thing led to another, and at the close of this delightful evening, my little lady insisted that she ring up her home, and the conversation ended with an invitation for me to visit with her family for a few days. I didn't have too much trouble parting with Walter, and I assured him I would be back to our tournament trail after my British-type weekend (Thursday through Monday). Since the Haig was always interested in the fairer sex himself, he welcomed my departure, and so started one of the most unforgettable ten days of my life.

Her "home" turned out to be none other than the sultan of Jahore's fabulous palace. It floated in the reflection of a small lake, and the whole scene overwhelmed me as we drove through the gates and through luxurious gardens to the entrance. Inside, I felt I had stumbled upon a massive jewel box. Gold chandeliers decorated halls studded with diamonds, rubies, and sapphires, with inlays of semiprecious stones. Fine satins and silks upholstered the furniture throughout, and the whole affair overlooked a large, almost olympic-sized swimming pool. Both inside and out, this modest swimming hole was fashioned with an intricate mosaic pattern of pink quartz and lapis lazuli. In entirety the palace was a tremendous work of art and overwhelming in its beauty.

To my surprise, I learned that the sultan was married to an Australian girl and that it had been her idea for me to "date" their daughter. Up to the moment when I met her parents, I had had no idea that I had been squiring such an important miss. In introducing me to his wife, the sultan said, "I'm sure you two will get along like next of kin, and it will be pleasant for my wife to have one of her own countrymen for a guest. Please make my humble palace your headquarters, and stay as long as you like. My family and I are very honored to have you here."

Only in the East would life hold such surprises. The Australian-born sultana then led the way up a large curving stairway to a suite of rooms with a balcony overlooking the garden and swimming pool. I was given what was known as the "Jade Suite," and real Chinese jade it appeared to be, too. My rooms were luxuriously furnished, with exquisite teakwood and priceless Persian rugs cushioning the floor. At every step I sank ankle-deep in euphoria. What the actual octane rating of a sultana is, I really don't know. In some countries the meaning is concubine. In ivy-league language it would mean just plain mistress. In Jahore, one of the Malay States, for the sultan to have many sultanas was a proud badge, a symbol of great success and prestige. However, in this case, the sultan's western wife had changed the tradition. She was extremely jealous of her husband—and rightly so—and it made for lively times.

The following day my host offered me a very tempting deal. Golf instruction in exchange for the charming young daughter, whom I'd begun to care for more than I should. What's more, to my surprise, I found that the sultan's private course was exceptionally fine. Only nine holes, but with lush carpetlike turf and a good test of skill. It was on high ground, and for caddies he had several young elephants to tote the clubs. At every hole there was a thatched-roof halfway house with attendants waiting to serve refreshments. And even the tee markers were unique, dazzling blue for the men and passionate pink for the ladies. Pretty appropriate thinking, I'd say.

The sultan's golf swing was absolutely horrible, so bad that I had to tear it apart and start from the bottom to build it again. I explained that patching it up as some teachers do would never really straighten him out; once I was gone, he'd revert to his old habits. So we started from the beginning.

I started my coaching by having the sultan stand comfortably and naturally, with his feet no wider apart than when he was talking casually to me. I told him the benefits of relaxation, keen timing, and, most important of all, follow-through. After my capsule explanation, my pupil started to improve right away. I stressed that he should stand more upright in his swing. Being rather slight in height, he bent over the ball trying to overpower it. But the clue is to stand up straight, not to stoop down over the shot. That way you can't "top" it but will be in the proper hitting position whether you watch the ball or not. I urged him to keep his head fairly still throughout the swing, but not necessarily "down." I stressed that it was a good thing for the head to move in keeping with the body action laterally. The hands, arms, and club must travel as far as possible on the line of flight. This same principle applies to every club in the bag, from the putter all the way up to the driver. To prove the point, I showed him what would happen to his putts if he didn't allow the putter head to travel in the direction of the hole.

After some immediate improvement in my host's game after just a few lessons, he begged me to stay on. "At least," he insisted, "until after the dinner party I am planning for Saturday night." I didn't need too much coaxing, for I was living life to the fullest, and accepted.

The festive evening came all too quickly. Many of the local rubber-plantation owners and their wives had been invited to attend. It was a very colorful event, and all the guests brought sons and daughters who were of age, for the social life was removed from the city and limited. All the guests were exquisitely attired in their finest clothes; the dowagers had bedecked their gowns with jewels, and the younger ladies wore their freshness as their beauty. Saris and ball gowns blended with the men in their black ties.

When we reached our seats at the dinner table, I found myself next to our hosts, with my princess and constant companion on my right. As a generous gesture in the form of a party favor for each lady, our host had placed a gift package from Paris at her place. There was a buzz of conversation about the contents of the gifts. The sultan rose and said that he wished his guests to dine, and before the dessert the ladies were to open their presents. He explained that he had bought them on his recent trip abroad and wanted them to enjoy this small remembrance as a token of his esteem.

Our dinner was sumptuous, with endless courses of game meat, rice, and tender green vegetables served with the finest European wines. The servants scurried in and out, hardly noticeable, but we were constantly urged to enjoy and taste. When the guests had finished the entrees, an orchestra was invited in, the plates cleared, and bowls of fruit and candied sweetmeats were heaped in front of each guest. Then, with a role of drums, our host invited the ladies to open their gifts. To everybody's merriment, what lay beneath each wrapping was a startlingly new swimming suit! It was truly the forerunner of the single-size stretch bikini, and with a multitude of twitterings the ladies all headed toward the changing rooms and the pool.

Of course, it was full night time by now, and the lights played on the numerous fountains that filled and fed the pool. The air was alive with tropical fragrance, and soon there was frolicking and playful laughter coming from the swimmers. The men meanwhile had been urged to stroll out on the balcony to smoke their cigars and tell a story or two. It seemed a good arrangement, and I was listening to the guffaws while trying to judge and select a beauty queen from the bathers below. After about ten minutes the sultan looked at his watch and beckoned all the men to the railing. It was just about then that the gifts, the new bathing suits, started to melt! They entirely disintegrated in the water!

And there they were, young and old, all sizes and shapes, trapped in the nude in the pool for our amusement. Well, I've never heard such shouts in my life. Complete pandemonium reigned, as some tried to hide by submerging or splashing and others by swimming and kicking vigorously. Goggle-eyed, we men finally tore ourselves away from the "new look" in swimsuits so that the ladies could come out. But we agreed that it was a style we heartily appreciated.

That evening ended my stay with the sultan. When it came time for me to be on my way the following day, he presented me with a book describing his many treasures, which now rests in the museum in Jahore. It was quite an adventure, a memorable interlude in my life. But I am convinced that there exists the world over a universal basic brotherhood common to all. For golfers seldom go their way alone. There are no barriers of breeding, color, or creed. A golfer is judged by his character, conduct, and deeds, and the sultan further proved to me that golfers are brothers.

HOLY COW

India was another happy hunting ground—wild game, that is—for Walter Hagen. Since there was always a way to arrange a bit of leisure between our matches and exhibitions, and the Haig expressed a burning desire to shoot a tiger, we arrived in Calcutta with but one thought in mind. Bagging the big cat is not an easy thing to do. The animal is large and strong and very fierce, as well as elusive. If there is a man-eating tiger threatening a village in India, the authorities write to a central office in Calcutta, and any hunter interested can use this as his source of information. Naturally, Walter made these inquiries and received word that there had indeed been a number of killings, and so we made immediate plans to get started for the shoot.

We were soon off, equipped with rifles and ammunition, provisions of all kinds, several bottles, and even a native guide. First we found the district and then the specific area where the animal had actually struck. After surveying the countryside, our guide built a "tree rest," essentially a large comfortable platform with room for us to put down blankets and stretch out. The next task was to get bait. It seemed that we had merely to buy an old cow, tie her to a fairly long rope, tie the rope to a tree, and after that climb into the "rest," pull the ladder up behind the last man, and wait until darkness, when the tiger would strike.

To make it even a bit more unfair, we had a flashlight on the rifle, synchronized with the gunsight. When the light picked up the target, all one had to do was pull the trigger. I'd never seen that kind of rig before. Just as soon as all this was made ready, up the tree the three of us went to wait for darkness and the tiger. Soon enough night started coming on, with blackness enclosing the whole landscape, and we waited and waited and waited for the sounds below. Time dragged and near three o'clock Hagen, who by this time was pretty tight, decided that he would take a nap. Without too much interest in the killing part of this caper, I too fell asleep, and finally the guide made it a threesome. When we awoke in the morning, our cow was gone. Tree, rope, animal —all had disappeared with practically no sign of a struggle. In fact, we followed the tracks to make sure that no human had set the bait free, but we could clearly trace the marks where the animal had been dragged away from the tree, down a bank, up the other side, and away. There was no doubt about the tremendous strength of that tiger. He had to be a large one—swift, silent, and strong—and this really challenged Walter.

Hagen couldn't believe his eyes, but he realized that he had lost his target. All he could say was, "Holy cow, how could that happen?" Naturally he was absolutely undaunted and now more determined than ever to get his sights on that cat. Nothing would do but for us to find another old beast of the field and tie her up for a fresh tantalizer. Hopes were high that he would score the second time around.

On this try Walter decided to use a chain, a metal link line, to tie the cow to the tree. He didn't want to take any chances on missing, and so at dusk up we went again to our perch to wait out the night. And wait we did most all that night, but eventually we all grew too tired and slipped off to sleep, mumbling that we were "just shutting our eyes for a doze." Again in the morning our cow was gone! The tiger must have come about daybreak and with a swift cuff made his kill and dragged his feast away.

Well, we tried it once more, again with no success. However, during that night Hagen was evidently bitten by a dangerous type of mosquito, because he soon grew very ill with a high fever. It turned out that he had contracted a bad case of black-fly malaria, and although he had taken quinine and all sorts of preventatives, I ended up taking him to the hospital. It was a close call for a while. Walter was delirious, and I didn't think he would make it, but the doctors gave him a treatment that burned the fever out of him, and his recovery was slow. For several months he was drained dry and had to lie low.

SURABAJA TO RANGOON

While my partner was resting and getting his strength back, I felt that I had to work some and try to keep a bit of money in the till. So I did a stint of independent traveling and exhibiting in Burma, India, and Ceylon. One unique course I played during that time was at Surabaja, Java. And what a strange one it was. The golf club and the local cemetery were a combined corporation. For a reasonable initiation fee, one not only became a lifetime member of the golf club but also was entitled to an "evermore membership" in the nineteenth hole, "that nasty big bunker of no return." The golfers had full and unlimited privileges of and to and in the cemetery. The deceased members of the club had even more permanent use of the links (in a rather confined, limited way). It was a mutually satisfactory arrangement for all concerned.

The entire nine-hole golf course completely surrounded the cemetery. You played over, in, and around the graveyard all the way. Dodging tombstones was a pretty good test of golfing—and tempers too. Let's say there were some bad lies, and liars, both in and off the course. I was bemused by a sign reading, "Divot Diggers are respectfully requested to avoid destroying or damaging the Daisies." The course, however, was in excellent condition with good grass greens, tees, and fairways. To score well one had to have complete control over the ball or be just dumb lucky, with the likelihood of a shot bouncing off the tombstone of some departed nineteenth holer. Let's just say that for golfers it was their own heaven. They had the satisfaction of being close to their buddies and would, in a small, warm way, cherish being part of the golf course forever.

The next few weeks passed rather peacefully. Then I landed an engagement to play at the Royal Golf Club in Rangoon. Aside from my love of the sport of golf, by this time it must be clear that I was an inexhaustible sightseer. Wherever my travels took me, I tried to educate myself in the wonders of the world, so endless in their beauty and historical interest. On this occasion I arrived a day ahead of my scheduled show and was told that there was a fantastic temple, the Shwe Dagon Pagoda, not to be missed.

The outside of the pagoda was an unforgettable sight, completely covered with gold leaf contributed by the people of Burma for their god. This covering had been laid on by men as an act of merit, and the building was spectacular to see. It consisted of many spired shrines rising in tiers, surrounding a central tower set on the hilltop dominating the whole city of Rangoon.

Local custom was to leave one's shoes at the door of the temple; it is against the Buddhist religion to walk on leather. Upon entering the building, I gave my eyes a while to adjust to the interior light, in contrast to the fantastic brilliance of the gold and sunshine outside. As I grew accustomed to the dimmer sanctum, I noticed that many Buddhas of every size

71

were scattered about as separate shrines. While rummaging around, I was naturally drawn to the largest statue of all, a massive seated image with a heavenly half-smile on its mouth. At his feet was an amazing collection of gifts of sacrifice—the strangest assortment of pots and pans, vegetables and flowers, furniture, things rare and common, large and small, all dwarfed by the huge, towering figure.

As I was examining these gifts, my eyes suddenly stopped with a jolt. What should I see in the midst of this conglomeration but an old picture of the Haig taken at St. Andrews during his first British Championship in 1920! I just couldn't believe it—the coincidence of this picture turning up here made me feel weird. Then a touch of avarice overcame me. I would give anything if that gift could be mine. I just salivated with the thought of the story I'd tell to the Haig. What a fine offering he'd made!

I had been told that it was the custom for the yellow-robed monks to go out of the temple and beg for their daily food. In the evening they evidently made a collection of all that was left at the foot of the Buddha, and they lived off it. Carefully looking all around, I realized that I was completely alone, and a seed was planted in my mind.

I figured that if I too made an offering, one better than this old battered picture, the Buddha would be ahead, and I might take that photo for a lesser exchange. Since it was still late afternoon and the marketplace would be filled with merchants, I headed down to the bazaar stalls with the thought that perhaps a bag of potatoes or some other foodstuffs would fill the bill. I set out for one of them.

Sure enough, I hadn't reached halfway downtown when I passed a vendor selling vegetables and fruit, and I bought his largest sack of ripe mangoes. I also had a goodly assortment of various change in my pocket, a collection from several countries. Armed with these two gifts, I returned to the pagoda. I decided to wait just inside the entrance until it became a little dimmer inside, yet not so late as to bump into those saffron-robed men.

As the afternoon passed, I began growing more and more nervous, even questioning the right and wrong of this exchange. But the time finally came when the temple was again deserted, and I stole into the center pavilion, putting my gifts at the crossed feet of the large Buddha while it seemed to stare down at me from exalted heights through the shafts of light and shadow. With a shaking hand, worse than a long putt for a championship, I put all the coins in a neat pile, placed the mangoes dead center, and swiftly grabbed up the battered old picture and hid it beneath my jacket. I moved quietly and swiftly out of there, so fast in fact that it was three blocks before I realized that I was shoeless. A casual observer might have confused me with an escapee from a bank robbery, but my real quandary now was whether to go back for my shoes or leave them there as a further offering.

Well, I had my picture all right. I'd torn my coat and lost my shoes in getting it, but I really felt that it was a fair bargain and didn't want to tempt the gods and buddhas above with any return performance. In fact, the next day I didn't even tell my hosts at the golf club about my experience but played my match and show and left for Mandalay with my precious prize in my satchel.

RACE-TRACK RAMBLE

Soon after my visit to Rangoon I experienced a rather serious accident—breaking my shoulder while playing some exhibition shots on an out-of-the-way course. All of which led me prematurely back to India to see how Walter was progressing and to check on our finances. Money matters were pretty shaky then, with cash dwindling, and for a period I couldn't contribute to our pot.

So there we were back in Calcutta, two disabled golfers, Hagen with lingering malaria and I with a big cast on my left side. Fortunately for me, I had met and found a great and good friend in John Nethersole, secretary of the Indian Horse Racing Committee and Jockey Club. He had a bungalow perched on the top of the grandstand at the track—a sort of penthouse that he offered to me for my use as long as I needed it. In return for his kindness, I coached him in his golf, which he practiced in the middle of the running field through the week (races were held only on Sunday). John was from New York State, and he was responsible for our invitations to exhibit in India and had set up the arrangements for us, on top of which he was personally a dedicated golf nut.

I should back up here to explain that after I was hurt I went to a local doctor to find out what damage I'd actually done to myself. He didn't think anything serious was wrong and waved off X-rays. He theorized that I'd just pulled a muscle, and sent me to a masseur, suggesting a series of workouts, rubs, and hot baths. Let me say that the massages nearly killed me; the pain was almost unbearable. While I was at the health club, I noticed that the jockeys regularly frequented the establishment to take steam baths. In time the proprietress got to know the riders pretty well, and I jokingly started kidding her one day, challenging, "You must get a lot of good tips on the races! I'll wager the real inside scoop."

She agreed. "Yes, I do, but I never follow any of them up. In fact, just the other day one of the fellows gave me the names of three horses, and he told me that whenever they ran to bet on them."

Not wanting to act too eager, I asked her with a chuckle, "Would you mind giving the names to me?" And she did.

I continued the treatments, but the pain became so severe that I had to give in and go to the hospital. This time the doctors did take X-rays and found that my shoulder was broken. For three weeks it had not only gone unset, but was being manipulated and massaged! They settled my situation by putting me in a thirty-seven-pound body cast, and back I went to my penthouse bungalow. Since I was incapacitated, time passed very slowly for me. But one of my diversions became the horses. I noticed that because of the intense heat of the day, the stable boys did all their training, time clocking, and exercising at night. Many a moonlit evening I would sit in my perch and watch the horses being put through their paces, all the while guarding those three names in my pocket.

After a week or two Walter was invited to visit one of the maharajas in the north. The air and temperature were far better in the mountains than at the coast, and by now he was making a steady recovery. I'd gone up to spend a few days in this exotic household. Then I noticed in the paper that my special threesome was running on the same bill that very next Sunday. I decided that it was time for a change for us, and I arranged to go to Calcutta for the meet. I next booked boat passage to Rangoon in order to pick up our playing schedule. Walter agreed to rendezvous with me in Burma in a week's time, and all seemed settled.

As it turned out, that race meet was a particularly large one. Some special memorial event was running, and the crowd numbered in the thousands. One of the special features of the celebration was a daily double hooked up to a treble. One could buy a combination ticket covering the first three races, as well as make individual bets. To top things off, all three names that I'd held so long were running in the first races. Gathering my courage, but nevertheless still rather cautious, I put a few rupees, about thirty, on the first horse, and to my surprise and delight he came in, paying 15 to 1. Not only that, but I'd got the first leg of the daily double. Now I figured I had a little money to spend on the second horse, a 20 to 1 shot. I put all my winnings from the previous race on him, and he won easily. Well, there was no doubt now that I had a pot of money. I mentally took count. I'd won the daily double and the individual races, and the third race had my horse rated an underdog at 5 to 1. The odds were on the favorite, supposedly unbeatable.

Playing it cool, I took my winnings and put all of them on the favorite to come in second. Meanwhile, I held my uncollected daily treble ticket, and I thought that was a pretty smart piece of hedging, to bet the favorite to place. That way I could collect for him to some degree and wouldn't risk everything on either the odds or my inside information.

The race stewards blew their bugles, and the horses walked from the paddock to the track. The jockeys jogged their mounts alongside the stands on their way to the starting gate. It was the longest race of the day, a mile and a half, and the excitement bubbled inside me. They were off and running. My horse, the 5 to 1 shot, and the favorite ran neck and neck at the start, both jockeys belting the hell out of their animals. When they rounded the turn, I almost lost sight of them, but the announcer kept repeating that these two were inches apart and drawing well ahead of the field. On the far turn the riders were trying to block each other's horses and were committing every breach in the book. But as they came into the straightaway finish, the horses separated and were running neck and neck, ear to ear, nostril to nostril, and I was almost dying.

As they came up to the winning post, my horse surged ahead with an incredible thrust of his neck, and it looked as though he was the winner. But before the results were announced, a protest was registered by the other jockey— all of this over the loudspeaker system since they didn't have a fancy electric board. Well, the inquiry lasted for a half-hour, and I knew that I had perhaps the only ticket on the treble, besides which I had the carryover of the "double" from the previous week because there hadn't been a winner. Furthermore, I had the ticket for the favorite for place. Never had time weighed so heavily. Well, a half-hour (or century, I should say) later they announced the winner, and it was my horse. I'd won $37,000, absolutely the whole thing, every bet I'd made. I couldn't believe it.

In India race-track earnings were normally taxable at about 50 per cent, and although it was Sunday, the collection boys were made aware of the big winners. Before I went down to collect my loot, I made a dash up to my apartment and emptied one of my suitcases, dumping the contents on the bed, and tore down to the payoff window.

Mind you, nobody knew that I'd won that much money, not my friend Nethersole or anyone else. The cashiers were reluctant to give me such a large amount of cash and suggested issuing a check to cover my winnings. But I insisted that I wanted it then and there and handed them my empty suitcase. Let me say that $37,000 in rupees is a lot of paper, but I'd already decided that I would make a run for the boat that very night. We were due to sail at eight the next morning, and I knew that none of the government offices opened until nine o'clock. I wanted to enjoy all the fruits of my betting and not share them with the tax department. It seemed to me that our need was greater at that moment. In fact, we were dead dry out of funds.

Whether it's betting on horses or making friends, it's the finish that counts. I made it a point to say my salaams to John Nethersole and his wife, Arlene, at the racing club. Then, pulling a handful of bills out of my newly stuffed suitcase, I beat it to the penthouse, grabbed my things, and was out of there in a matter of minutes. You've never seen such a fast departure in your life.

I didn't really feel I'd pulled it off until the next morning when the ship was safely out in the middle of the Indian Ocean. It wasn't until then that I breathed a sigh of relief and started to think ahead.

As for Walter, when I unpacked my suitcase in front of him several days later, he couldn't believe his eyes. "Ah,

Joe Kirkwood, age eighteen, golf professional at Riverside Golf Club, Ashburton, Australia

NOTE: *Legends for the illustrations were prepared by Ron Kirkwood, Joe Kirkwood's son*

Kirkwood after winning the Australian Open and New Zealand Championship, Australia, 1920

Victor East (left) and Kirkwood on a stop-over at Pinehurst, North Carolina, on their way to England

Kirkwood putting on the second green at the Open Golf Championship, St. Andrews, Scotland

The eighteenth green, Lossiemouth Tournament, Scotland, won by Kirkwood, May 17, 1922

Kirkwood versus Abe
Mitchell, Gleneagles £1,000
Tournament, 1921

Kirkwood with the Lossie-
mouth Tournament Trophy,
which he won by thirteen
strokes over George Duncan
in Scotland, 1922

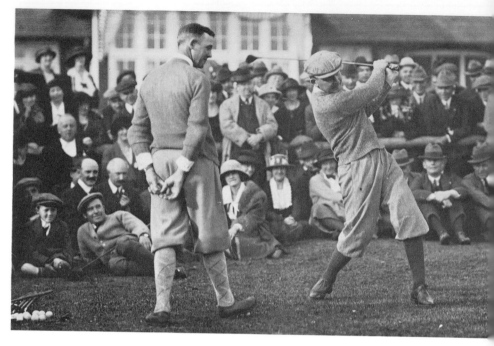
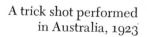

Kirkwood (right) hitting a ball off a spectator's foot in an exhibition in Australia

A trick shot performed in Australia, 1923

Kirkwood practicing stymie shots on a putting green in San
Francisco, 1922

Foreground, left to right: Walter Hagen, Kirkwood, Gene Sarazen, and Johnny Farrell, photographed in the mid-1920's

Henry Cotton (left)
and Kirkwood
(right), Isle of Man,
1927

Hagen (left) and Kirkwood, St. Louis, Missouri

Kirkwood and friends, Australia, 1935

Kirkwood (left) at a
boomerang-throwing
lesson, Australia

Kirkwood (left) in South America with Sarazen, 1934

Hagen and Kirkwood (right) in South Africa, 1937

Hagen teaching South African natives to shimmy, 1937

Hagen shooting craps with natives in Southern Rhodesia

A Tanganyika "caddie," 1937

Kirkwood in India, 1935

Kirkwood playing a shot off an elephant, Celon, 1935

The Indians called him the "Wizard One," after he shot a course record of 55 at Madras, India, on April 8, 1935

Hagen in India

One of Kirkwood's many
trick shots—hitting two
balls with two clubs—
Madras, India, 1934

Kirkwood in Egypt, 1937

Hagen and Kirkwood racing around a pyramid, Egypt, 1937

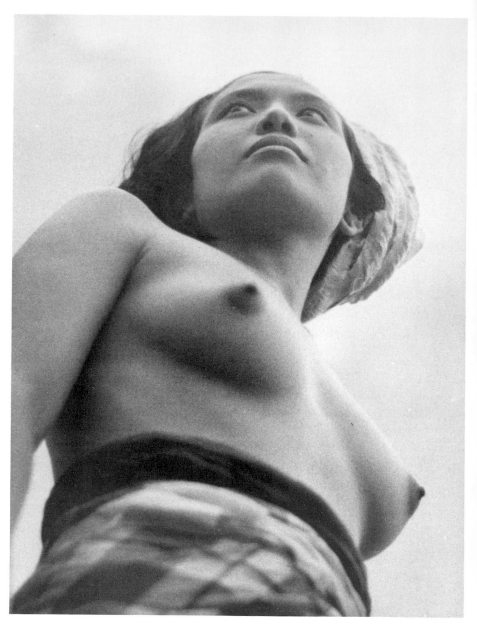

A Bali native girl

The Bali home of Le Mare, the Belgian artist

Le Mare's Balinese housemaid

A Balinese golf lesson

Kirkwood practicing trick shots on the beach at Bali, 1937

Kirkwood teaching golf to Japanese soldiers, 1938

Hagen (left) and Kirkwood, Hungjao, China, 1938

Hagen and Kirkwood in front of the hotel, Miyanoshita, Japan, 1930

The first tee, Ibaraki, Japan, May 25, 1930

Hagen, photographed in the early 1940's

Kirkwood performing at a golf exhibition before the Duke and Duchess of Windsor in the Bahamas (autographed "Wallis Windsor" and "Edward")

Kirkwood on his way to England, 1934

An exhibition in England, 1940

An exhibition at San Quentin Prison, San Francisco, California

Kirkwood entertaining servicemen at a military hospital, Atlanta, Georgia, during World War II

A golf exhibition in Pennsylvania, 1940's

Kirkwood imitating a beginner trying to hit a golf ball. Courtesy
Dick Hanley Photography, New York City

Kirkwood hitting
three balls
with three clubs
in an exhibition

Kirkwood's bag of clubs used in his golf exhibitions. Courtesy
Dick Hanley Photography, New York City

Kirkwood's tombstone. Joe died on October 30, 1970. "His friends do not remember how he died; they only remember how he lived"

Kirkie," he said, "now we can really live it up. Of course, I have a few unpaid bills back there which you can take care of. But now we can swing. 'Swing easy,' I always say!"

PART FOUR

BALI

One of the most delightful bits of wandering that I've ever enjoyed occurred during the rainy season in a most remote part of the Far East. It happened in the Dutch East Indies, not more than a long water hole off the coast of what was once Java, a Dutch possession, now Indonesia, on the island of Bali. I journeyed there to pay a long-delayed visit to an old Belgian friend named Le Marc. At that time this artist was an unknown obscure amateur, but today Le Mare is recognized as a successful island painter who exhibited both in the Orient and Paris.

It was my pleasure to be his guest during my stay at his extremely beautiful bungalow on the beach, about twenty miles from the town of Den-Pasar. He was more or less alone on this stretch of sand, and his rambling thatched-roof native cottage was very close to nature in its finest sense. There's no doubt that I was badly bitten by the Bali "fever," for it was here that I decided I had found the paradise that we all long for, but somehow find illusive in the busy commercial world.

The Balinese are a gracious people, the happiest and most carefree in the world, without problems or complexes. They are extraordinarily cheerful and genuinely friendly, and their manner and demeanor are like their language—soft-spoken and gentle. They are a wholesome and healthy race with simple native customs. Both men and women are naked from the hips up, wearing only colorful sarongs of hand-blocked batik. This fabric was woven and richly colored by the natives themselves. Speaking of the sarongs, I was amused to learn of the strait-laced influence of the missionaries, who attempted to change this lifelong custom of dress. It seems that they once tried to teach the girls and ladies of the land that it was immodest to expose their bosoms, particularly in the presence of Europeans. Consequently, from that time on, whenever the native girls happened to be passing any foreigners in their towns or villages, they would reach down and lift their sarongs to cover their bare breasts, thereby uncovering even more of their nakedness!

My host's cottage was unique unto itself, with his canvases as well as ancient wood carvings on every wall. Attached to the house was a patio where the natives daily left flowers. In the midst of all this was his studio, where three flawless native women lived and posed as models of voluptuous perfection. They were perfectly beautiful people who took pleasure in every day, and their smiling dispositions were like the sun itself.

In the evening the atmosphere became even more dreamlike, with the changing patterns of light and shade playing on colors of the forest and sea, and these lovely girls to do our bidding. I know I struck it off with them because they soon fitted me out with a sarong, which I wore when searching the sands for precious shells and even during my practice golf shots which I had started to hit from the beach to a nearby abandoned rice field.

I laid out a pretty nice little course, and since I didn't want to get too rusty, I found myself swinging the clubs regularly. Somehow word of my activities spread, because after a few days a neighboring plantation owner came by and asked if I would give a show for the islanders, assuring me that the natives and the farmers would be both enthusiastic and interested. Of course, I agreed and arranged to do the performance out on the field which I christened The Ti-Ti Golf Club. I simply sank some tin cans in the ground, fashioned some flags, and cleared several flat spots for tees.

By smoke signal or word of mouth, folks came in droves from far and wide to attend the gala day. Most of them had never heard of or seen a golf shot, but these people turned out in numbers for almost all events—cock fights, weddings, feasts, and such. Nevertheless, it was gratifying to see such a large and enthusiastic group materialize from nowhere. And although I didn't speak their language, I did communicate with them, because the show was received with much laughter and delight. Furthermore, I'll have to confess that it was there in Bali that I devised one of my most successful trick shots and added it to my repertoire.

Goggle-eyed with the crowd, I found myself looking in the direction of my sarong-gowned gallery instead of at the ball, and I got surprisingly good results. I said to myself, "To hell with keeping my head down and gazing at the ground when there's such a tremendously warm and natural sight ahead." Then and there I decided to hit golf shots looking out at that bevy of Balinese instead of following the age-old theory of "keeping the eye on the ball."

When I was finished, a stately gentleman, a native Balinese, approached me and asked in perfect English whether

85

I would consider teaching his daughter to play golf. He explained that she was to be traveling to the mainland for college in a few months and that he would like her to have a little knowledge of the sport. I found out later that he was a prominent person, very wealthy, important, and of the Balinese aristocracy. I asked whether the young lady had any clubs, and he answered that he would order some from Surabaja. They arrived by boat about a week after our conversation.

Some days later at an appointed hour, I went out to the field where I'd set up my golf holes. I hadn't waited long when the most beautiful young woman that I'd ever seen approached me, wearing only her sarong. Completely stunned, I felt my pulse accelerate. There I was, asked to give golf lessons to one of the most voluptuous creatures I'd ever put eyes on, and she was topless.

To say that it was hard to concentrate would be putting it mildly. Her gorgeous body gleamed in the sunlight, and watching her put to use my instruction was a study in anatomy—hers and mine. After the initial surprise, I pulled my wits together and realized that, since she had never been introduced to the sport, I had to start at the very beginning. It was an amazing way to be able to test my theories. After showing her a proper stance and grip, I had her extend her arms out and hold her hands away from her body, rather than having them low in her lap. I showed her the advantage of not breaking the unit of arms to club, thereby minimizing the margin of hitting error. In all, I explained that I wanted her to have a total fluid motion, but connected, from hands to arms and shoulders, turning and moving with her hips, legs, and feet, all smoothly together like a dance.

With only the scantiest knowledge of English, she caught on to all of this very quickly and progressed as rapidly as any pupil I'd ever had. She was soon hitting her short irons with accuracy and even skill, and she was consistent too, standing and swinging in a natural way. Aside from that, her grace and manner became so endearing that each day as she would prepare to leave me for her home, my eye lingered longer and longer on her disappearing form as she walked serenely away through the foliage to some private path.

Late one afternoon at the end of the lesson, she looked up at me announcing, "Joe, I have a gift for you."

I couldn't imagine what it could be, but my admiration for her as a person and for her beautiful young body had totally captured and tantalized me. With a slight movement, she placed her hand in mine and cajoled, "Come, follow me. It is just the right time."

She must have been watching me over those past weeks, not only during the lessons but afterward, when I thought I was alone, scanning the beaches for rare shells and bits of coral. When I followed her, she led me to a cove where she had a canoe. With incredible speed we pushed out from the shore and were on our way to an island a short distance off. She said that it was "her island, her secret place," and that she was giving it to me to share together because of the gifts I'd given her. As we approached the small coral atoll, I was struck with its incredible glow of pink. The rays of the sun struck it in such a way as to make it haloed in an unreal and vibrant color. When we beached our dugout, I found the shores of that tiny place covered with gorgeous shells. She left me, laughing and saying that I was to explore her present and then come to find her.

I soon discovered that, set back from the shore of the island, was the richest growth of tropical trees, temple flowers, and foliage that I'd ever seen. No one had tried to tame or clear any part of it, and towering tree ferns with clusters of orchids clinging to their trunks lay neighbor to frangipani and fragrant vanilla vine; gingerblooms and flame bushes, reaching like bright red torches to the sky, crowded together next to the banyan and breadfruit trees. I was overwhelmed, like an ersatz Robinson Crusoe, and set out to find my companion. At that moment I didn't care about shells or the sunset or anything; my whole body was aching for her. And it didn't take me long to find her. Inland from our landing place I stopped dead in my tracks at the sounds of splashing and tumbling water. There was my Polynesian lass, swimming like a dolphin, completely nude in an inner lagoon that was filled with the ocean waters at high tide. The sea was captured, and so was she, in all her sweetness and innocence. My laughing native miss grew very dear to me, and her trust and enjoyment in life gave me a whole new outlook on the world.

We returned to her island many times over the next few weeks. She showed me bamboo groves where all the birds nested, bougainvillaeas, and azaleas, vines all growing in wild profusion, and even fruits ripe and unharvested in their natural surroundings. But her freshness and fragrance bloomed like the flowers around her, and I was being torn apart trying to decide what my future should be. Somehow she sensed this because, just before a short trip that I was making away from Bali, my hosts planned a special departure feast and celebration. Perhaps they knew that I wouldn't return, though they never said as much.

On the evening before the small packet boat was to arrive, I donned my specially made new sarong and was treated to a fantastic and memorable meal. A roasted suckling pig, baked in the special Balinese way with pineapples and mangroves, was preamble to the temple dancers. They were dressed in their traditional, fabulous costumes, made entirely of woven eighteen-carat gold studded with semi-precious stones. The girls had come from all over the island, and their dance in the firelight made a special dream of the night. The strangely beautiful fleeting music played by gongs and tiny bells still lingers in my memory and always will. That evening—in that moment of time—and the soft smile of Bali would be with me forever.

HALTING A WAR

Surely one of our most memorable matches—even historic, you might say—also took place in the Orient. Walter and I had just made the big swing down and around from Australia to Singapore and Manila, when I received an invitation to play at the Hung Jao course in Shanghai. The year was 1938, at the height of the Sino-Japanese War. The town of Shanghai was a shambles, but the local golf association was still operating, even though the Japanese authorities had taken over the country club for one of their command posts. The international settlement, however, was protected. British, Italian, German, and Russian diplomats and business people were all living amid fierce fighting, bombs falling, and disruption about them.

We thought that the invitation was so unique that we couldn't resist the trip, and we arrived in that shattered city full of curiosity about how we could put on our show. Our hosts had arranged to house us comfortably at the picturesque and elegant Cathay Hotel, one of the few hotels still standing. It was situated by the Hwang Pu River, which was jammed with people and commerce and sometimes turned scarlet from the blood of those dying from the bombs dropped wide by the Chinese Nationalists.

We found to our astonishment that in our honor the Japanese and Chinese had called a truce to the fighting for a day. We literally halted the war while the two enemies paused to watch our exhibit, posting a sign that called for the "Golfers of Shanghai to Gather at the Club" for the match and requested the authorities to clear the dead bodies from the course. The Orientals never picked up their dead or wounded. They were either too busy or life was too cheap, and they just stacked them in the ditches and lagoons. The smell was absolutely terrible, a foul deal.

To make the whole scene a bit more challenging, a bomb had fallen the day before, destroying the last green. A temporary sand green was hastily constructed on the eighteenth hole so that all was seemingly repaired in time for our play.

Well, we did the show, and the Chinese and Japanese officers were packed side by side in the gallery watching. It was an amazing affair for us. They seemed polite and cordial, and didn't appear to feel that their behavior was the least bit unusual. In the late afternoon the ladies arrived to serve tea, the embroidered-silk *chang-sam* gowns of the Chinese women mixing with the kimonos and obis of the Japanese; The Western ladies were the picture of chic, contrasting with the servants, who floated among us with Oriental quiet in long white gowns and black vest jackets. The scene was festive and cosmopolitan and gracious, totally incongruous to any hostility.

Following refreshments, everyone gathered to watch my exhibition. They seemed delighted and intrigued with the performance, which I had worked up to a fine pitch. First of all, I placed seven balls on tees in a line and drove them off with a steady swing, perfectly straight, without a second's hesitation between shots. The only hitch was that, as I aimed at one ball, I actually hit the one next to it. Next I embedded a ball in the turf and used my brassie to send the white pellet about two hundred yards away. Then followed my various iron shots, and I showed a variety of effects high and low, sliced and pulled, and I demonstrated how a ball could be hit to travel accurately with a low trajectory and then soar like a swooping swallow.

The show progressed with my drive from a one-footed stance. Then I placed one ball over another and drove the bottom ball straight down the fairway while the topmost ball dropped onto the tee. I sent the next one from the shined toe of the boot of an unsmiling Japanese officer standing nearby and then asked him to lend me his pocket watch to use for a tee on my next shot. Following that, I played two balls, positioned a few inches apart, as one, with two clubs in hand, making one ball slice while the other curved to a hook. For the finale, I hit golf balls down the fairway at a caddie, sending a shower of low-line balls zinging by his head, making him duck and feint and flounder every which way.

When it was all over, the Japanese officers seemed to be in a huddle of conversation. Finally, with an abrupt stride, the senior officer came up to me and asked if I would repeat the last series for them. He said that that particular routine had interested them the most of all the maneuvers. I agreed, saying that it would be no trouble. This seemed to please them and resulted in a series of commands to some of the enlisted men standing nearby and created a scurry of activity.

What they actually did was to dress some Japanese privates in Chinese uniforms and send them down behind the distant bunkers (which were, in fact, early graves). At one time the whole golf course had been a farm, and in old China they buried their dead anywhere as long as it wasn't under the ground. Instead, they put the bodies on top of the surface and piled the soil in a mound on top of them. Seasons passed, and these burial mounds became grassed over and were what were later used as bunkers. (It was not unusual after a rainstorm to see bones protruding from the earth, washed out by the moisture and shifting soil.)

Following the exchange between the officers, the appointed five or six soldiers with bayonets and rifles "ready," were sent down the fairway, and I was asked to commence my play. They had instructed the men to charge toward me, while I hit low-flying, hard golf shots at them. I had them ducking and falling all over the place, frightened of being hit. When they came within thirty or forty yards of me, they'd had enough. They turned tail and ran back, their guns and swords clanking, and hid behind the bunkers.

Over the next two weeks I traveled with an American newsreel photographer named Gordon. We saw war at its worst, slipping from shelter to shelter taking pictures of the actual fighting. I'll never forget seeing prisoners tied to trees and posts, just left to die. The Japanese didn't return to take them down after capture. The human suffering and brutality was unbelievable.

Some time later, when I reached Japan, I found that the officers at Hung Jao that day had made a movie of the last scene of my show. They were using it as a propaganda stunt to illustrate the cowardice of the Chinese, how they would even turn their backs and run from a golf ball.

However, we couldn't become embroiled in the politics and economics of the various countries we visited to entertain. Our goals were to bring laughter, sport, and comradeship to people, and these objectives seemed to be universally appreciated.

Continuing with our tour to Kobe, Japan, we played an interesting match on a course whose fairways and greens were entirely covered with bentgrass (the grass used on the greens only in this country). It was there in Kobe that I hit a ball off General Tojo's shoe during my exhibition. Following this exotic experience we visited a club a good distance from Tokyo, where, midway around, the green on which we were putting started to wobble and then to shake violently. Even the golf balls began to quiver and move. I'll never forget Hagen. He scowled up at me while huddled over a putt and said, as if he wanted a confirmation of the fact, "Kirkie, we've left the shooting war, but this course is moving!" I agreed with him.

"Wow!" he said, looking relieved. "I thought my nerves were going."

There was a minor earthquake that day. The Japanese didn't take it very seriously, but we did. From "halting a war" to playing through earthquakes, we agreed that golf was weaving a fine thread through life, a life worth living for the two of us.

SOAKED IN SAKE

During our second trip to Japan, Walter and I felt that we were really gaining steam. We had the best galleries that we'd ever drawn, and everyone seemed enthusiastic about the tour. It was not only a success from the host's point of view but gratifying for us, too. The enthusiasm was catching.

With this kind of reception, there was little to quarrel with, except one requirement as far as the Japanese directors were concerned. That was for the matches to start right on time. The Japanese are a precise people, punctual and orderly, and they always stressed that we run our show on schedule. Right up to the last match (and we played over twenty of them) I was able to get us to the starting tee on time. This was a bit of a chore where Walter was concerned because he was a late riser, a relaxed fellow in every way, and liked to catch planes and trains when the wheels were turning, not to speak of arriving at a golf course at an exact starting time.

The final exhibition match and show were scheduled at

the Yokohama Country Club. Intricate plans were underway for a big farewell celebration and party, involving a lot
of planning and groundwork. Coincidentally, during our
visit Walter had become great and fast friends with Jimmy
Kawasaki, one of the most prominent and successful Japanese businessmen in the country and also president of the
Yokohama Golf Course. It was he who had put us up in
Oriental style at the Imperial Hotel, close by in Tokyo. On
the night before the final exhibition match, Jimmy decided
to take Walter out on the town, not only to the Ginza but to
a number of private parties as well. They cut quite a swath,
staying out late and drinking as they went, and as they
progressed they accumulated geisha girls. It is forbidden to
take these women out of an establishment, but one can have
them sent along afterward in a following cab. At the finish,
they had nineteen petite, painted geishas. I stayed with the
party as long as I could, but being a nondrinker, I finally quit
and went back to the hotel.

The next day dawned all too quickly for me, and I knew
that my major problem was to get Hagen to the exhibition.
Yokohama is about thirty-five miles from Tokyo, and I had
to allow some lead time for us to cover those extra miles out
to the club. About nine o'clock in the morning I heard a
heated conversation in the hall of the hotel, and who should
it be but Hagen, insisting that Jimmy Kawasaki stay "the
night" with him. Needless to say, there was no "night" left,
but I didn't interfere with them, thinking that I'd let them
get some sleep before I had to rouse them for the big day.

At about 11:30 I decided that the sands had just about
run out and that it was time for me to take some action. I
started with Walter's room and, as I expected, he was completely passed out, all the way gone. The effects of the sake
were violent, and since he'd been in training, so to speak, he

was all the more vulnerable. I decided that perhaps the best solution would be to send up a masseur. It was probably the only way to bring him round. I made inquiries from the bell captain, and he arranged to send the house therapist to Walter's room on the double.

A burlier, hairier, larger Russian I had never seen. He was a giant of a man, and he started right in, pummeling Walter, kneading his flesh, and darn-near killing him. He succeeded to some small extent, because Walter finally woke up enough to complain about the operation. With instructions that I was leaving a car for him and arranging for Jimmy to drive him out to the club, I decided to get to the course and check in with the officials, showing polite timeliness.

When I arrived, the size of the crowd startled me. People had come from far and wide to view their new sports idols—us. Anticipating the worst, I went to the club committee and explained that Walter didn't feel too well and that he was with Jimmy Kawasaki. I suggested that I do my show first. They agreed that this might be a good way to hold the audience until Hagen's arrival, and so I began my routine. As a rule, my exhibition took about an hour and a quarter. Two hours and twenty minutes later I was still hitting balls, every shot I ever knew, and a lot I didn't know. I hit a drive with my putter (two hundred yards!), putts with my driver, pantomimes of lady golfers, blind shots, slices, hooks, stymie loops, my whole bag and more, and my hands were blistering—on the verge of bleeding.

Finally I saw some heads turn toward the clubhouse, and there was Walter weaving his way toward the first tee. With relief I closed off my entertainment and announced that the match they had looked forward to was about to begin. When I reached Hagen, I hissed under my breath, "Where the hell have you been?"

He answered with a grin, "I got stuck in a rickshaw jam, Kirkie."

With that we started off. The crowd (there must have been nearly 4,000 of them) struggled in to get a close look at the Haig, and when the caddie teed up Walter's ball, the big man sent his shot right out over those people's heads. I was sure he was going to kill someone, his aim was so erratic. But I knew that, once started, I couldn't stop the match. The people were there to see a hero, and it would have been far worse to call it off than to let Hagen struggle on. And struggle and stagger he did. He didn't even score a bogey, let alone a par. At the seventh hole, to compound his troubles, he had a strong call of nature. Sidling up to me, he questioned, "Gee, Joe, there aren't any outhouses around here are there?"

"Well," I suggested, looking around, "that looks like a shack out there in the rice paddy. Maybe you could slice your ball in that direction and try it for size."

However, instead of slicing, he pulled a horrendous hook. It really shook him because he had to go in the worst way. But a hole later he spied another rundown bunch of boards and speculated that this one really had to be an outhouse. To reach this structure, it was necessary to walk a plank path set between some barbed-wire fencing to a section of soaked paddy field well off the course. Walter evidently didn't feel that he had much of a choice. He made a wild dash for this hut, and when he ducked between the wire he scraped too close and tore a big patch right out of the seat of his brand-new silk golfing knickers. Undaunted, he made a lunge for the building and disappeared behind its flimsy door.

Meanwhile, we waited for his return. When he finally made his reappearance, the whole scene became frenzied. It seemed that he'd run right into the home of some nesting bees. They weren't at all happy about Walter disturbing their tranquillity and started to swarm about him. This sobered the old boy up in a hurry, and he got his business done and literally bombed out of that shack back onto the course.

I'll never forget the discreet politeness of the Japanese people in the crowd. One of the ladies who had witnessed the whole scene at close quarters softly stepped up and knelt on the green. Taking a large pin out of her obi she constructed a makeshift patch on the seat of Walter's pants. This considerably eased the embarrassment of the moment.

At the eleventh hole, which was ordinarily a drive and short chip but which on this day could be easily reached from the tee, Hagen's ball touched the narrow entrance to the green, only to kick down the bank of a small creek. Too strong with his second and woefully short with his third, he grumbled to me, "Kirkie, this must be a long hole."

"We're gaining on it," I answered, and ran my putt down for a par 4.

Further on at the fifteenth, I tried to add a bit of humor to break the mounting disappointment of his showing. I had a putt of about twenty-five feet, and the green lay partly on a hillside. With a firm grip I punched the ball uphill and let it roll back down the bank toward the cup. It lacked about a couple of inches of going in, and as I looked at its path I joked to the gallery, "That's one of my vices. I don't smoke and I don't drink, but I like short putts!"

The match was near the end now, and I'd never seen Walter fall down on the job before. But he didn't hit a decent shot during the entire round. Before or after the bees he had lost all of his sting, and this game was a beaut.

On the final green his ball lay at the outer fringe in eight. He must have had a seventy-foot putt to the cup, across an undulating surface with a sizable cross grain. Unpredictable as always, he started by in a big hurry toward the clubhouse. It looked as though he was going to pick up his ball, but instead, as he walked by, never looking down, he stroked away backhanded with his putter. To the gasps of the crowd, that final hit went dead-eye for the cup and in.

The caddie couldn't contain himself, and he hollered after the disappearing Walter, "Mr. Hagen, you sunk it! You holed out!"

With which Walter turned and, never looking at the pin or the ball at all, announced, "Hell, I knew that. I've never gotten a ten in all my life!"

HASTE YE BACK

Now back in Europe, the Haig and I found ourselves traveling once again. We'd been involved in some pretty funny bits of skulduggery, but one of the grandest spoofs that ever took place happened then, in bonnic Scotland, with my old barnstorming partner. On an off-morning, while we were meandering through the glens and winding byways, sightseeing that lovely land, our roaming led to events that included my taking a lesson from an old Scots golf professional.

We had stopped at several inns and pubs in search of a suitable place for lunch when finally we found a small-town golf club near Inverness that looked inviting. After inquiring, we learned that the dining room didn't serve luncheon on the Sabbath until 1:00 P.M. So, rather than move on, we decided to call a halt to our wanderings and hang around until chow time, the club being a rather pleasant place to linger awhile.

Walter, however, was suffering pangs produced by a large party the night before and was badly in need of some liquid refreshment. He soon found his way to the lounge, where he made himself known and was welcomed "in the only way Scotsmen know."

I became bored by being bar-based and decided to take a walk to look at the links. Watching my departure out of the corner of his eye, the Haig hollered, "Where are you going, Kirkie?"

"To take a golf lesson," I answered.

"Good," he quipped. "You'll need it with me in the future."

That remark gave me an idea. Knowing how Walter loved a laugh, this was as good an opportunity as any to give him one. On our way into the club, I'd spotted a golf shop a short distance down the hill from the main building. I headed my footsteps in that direction, curious to see what kind of equipment they had on display. Once there, I noted that all round the walls of the rustic pro shop was an assortment of clubs of every known kind, make, and vintage, all polished and placed neatly in their proper order.

Upon my entry, a meek old man emerged from the back room where he had been working at repairing clubs. A quiet little man, his face deeply suntanned, rugged, and wrinkled, somewhat resembled a sackful of busted shoelaces or belonged on a petrified prune. His large, roughhewn hands unmistakably were those of a golf player, weathered by the salty winds from the North Sea. A typical highlander, he had a cluster of lines around his kindly, deep-blue eyes, a sign of a cheerful person who laughed a lot, characteristic of the golf pros of that land as a result of a healthy life on the links. He welcomed me cordially in a rich Scots accent and asked if he could assist me. This nice gent had plenty of Old World courtesy, a quality rather sadly lacking in this day and age in the golf profession.

"I'm Jock Kilcauldie, but I'm nae kin of Andrew Kilcauldie of St. Andrews," he said.

I asked if I could look around for a while and he replied, "Take ye time, laddie."

I browsed and idled around the shop for a few minutes, picked up a left-handed mashie upside down, held it like an ax, and awkwardly tried to make it sit right-handed. Immediately the old man approached and explained that I had a left-handed club in my hands. I innocently asked, "What are all these sticks? That's really a strange assortment of shillelaghs you have here, mister." As I fingered them, I looked up at him and asked, "Do they actually use all these sticks in a game?"

Well, the old pro's blue eyes blazed indignance, and his bronzed face grew grim when I referred to the clubs as "sticks." That's a dirty word, worse than calling a fisherman's rod a "pole." When you call a golf club by such a common name in the presence of a Scotsman, you can only expect dirty looks. The game of golf in the land of haggis and heather is a religion, and its future is always somewhat mingled with the past. Like all his clansmen, this old-timer was a real pro with almost a sacred respect for the game of golf and everything pertaining to it. Golf to him was something more than a game; it was a lifelong ritual. This dour old character knew the code well and treasured the traditions, as all true Scots do.

I remarked, "Gosh, mister, you must sell a lot of these golfing sticks."

"Nae, laddie, I don't, but the salesman who sold them to me sells plenty." And again with a hurt expression he indignantly reminded me that they were not "sticks" but "gouf clubs," and he gave the name its true Scots pronunciation.

"Oh, I thought those things were some sort of hockey

stick, like they play with out my way in Canada, but they seem rather small and frail for that game."

He grinned happily. "Think nothing of it, laddie. I don't suppose the golf game has reached your part of the world yet. Canada, they tell me, is a pretty primitive country."

Posing as a cattleman from the faraway plains of Alberta, I told him that no such game was played where I came from and that I'd heard about it, but only vaguely. I put on a bit of a "that-a-way" accent. Feigning complete ignorance, I made out that I had never seen the game of golf played anywhere before. "It sure looks like fun," I added.

Eventually I got around to inquiring about what he did other than selling and repairing clubs. He replied, "I'm the professional here."

"Pardon my ignorance, but what does that mean?" I asked.

"I teach people to play the game."

"Your work?" I queried.

I received a nodded reply.

"My friend and I have a while to wait for lunch. Do you think I could take a shot at your game meanwhile?" I asked. "Maybe you could give me a quick lesson and teach me to play golf while I'm waiting for the dining room to open. How much do you charge to teach?"

"My fee for an oors lesson is one sovereign."

"Gee," I said, "I'd like to give it a go." In all seriousness I asked, "Couldn't I learn the game today?"

"Och, nay laddie, ye canna learn the gouf game in one lesson. It takes years, and with many people, never!"

He asked me if I knew anything at all about the sport. And I said, "Well, I believe you're supposed to hit a little white ball with a stick; then you have to try and find it and hit it over and over again until you find the hole."

He asked a lot of other questions too, but I played dumb to all of them. I confessed that I didn't even know which end of the caddy to use, "nor a bunker from a duffer." Innocently I inquired if golf playing was anything like "cricket or croquet." I thought the poor chap would go daffy at my stupidity; he must have been convinced that I had a "gap in my gourd." How he ever stuck it out I'll never know. But I paid him a pound in advance and promised to double it if he could teach me something about golf.

That did it. Right away the old Scot, true to his instincts, hauled out his ancient pocket watch (it looked more like an alarm clock), and studied it for a brief moment. "Maybe I can give you a lesson."

"Fine," I said. "It will be a new experience, and when I get back home, I'll be able to show my friends how to play."

"You don't have any equipment, do you?" he asked. He went out into the back room and brought a pail full of badly abused practice balls which I'm sure came from the Dark Ages. He also asked if I had shoes. This time I said, "Of course I do," pointing to my feet.

"Oh, pardon me," he said, "I mean golf shoes."

I expressed surprise. "Do I need a special outfit to do this thing?"

He assured me that it wasn't necessary, "But most folks do dress for golf in knickers, sweaters, cap and spiked golf shoes."

"I'll get those later," I said. "I'll learn to play first." However, I relented and purchased a new pair of golf shoes, which I needed anyway, but, being two sizes too big, they looked like gunboats on my feet. Nevertheless, I was all set for the first golf lesson of my life, which proved to be quite an exhausting experience.

The highlander's teaching technique was rather "oldtimish" in some respects, yet simple and sane, in keeping with the method used by the first Scots professionals, which later became obsolete. Their ways have since been drastically changed and greatly improved. When he asked me whether I was right- or left-handed, I gave a blank stare.

"Well," I said, "Actually, I don't know. Is there a difference?" Finally I suggested, "Let's try it both ways to make sure."

As I clutched the club with vise-like hands, I commented, "Gosh, Jock, this stick doesn't seem too sturdy. I hope I don't break it."

Again he reminded me that it wasn't a "stick" and that "it won't break either." Awkwardly I grasped the club like an ax handle, first with my fists, left-handed, cross-handed, then right-handed, even back-handed. Clumsily I worked both sides of each club, to no avail.

The pro looked at me with unspoken revulsion. I'm sure he wanted to say, "Son, you'd better find another game," but he refrained.

I turned to my teacher and confided, "I'm afraid, my good man, you have a real raw rookie on your hands. You'll have to be patient with me. I'm not too bright, nor am I any good at games. No time for that stuff on a farm, you know."

"Aye, ye'll be all recht," he assured me. This genial gent had the patience of a pope. Disgusted as the poor fellow undoubtedly was, he nevertheless continued to persevere with his impossible pupil. Strange as it may seem, this fine-faced fellow never at any time tumbled to what was happening. He hadn't the slightest inkling that I had ever golfed before. Since I was dressed in ordinary street clothes, felt hat, even trouser suspenders, he had no idea of my identity. Actually, there was little likelihood of him recognizing me, particularly without my sports attire. I looked like any other tourist or visitor to those shores. Furthermore, being more or less a stranger, very few people knew me, and I felt quite safe. My only judge was conscience. Later after I had left, I hated to think that I had hurt the kindly fellow's feelings.

Soon I was to hear howls of laughter from up yonder. The lounge was in an uproar of merriment. From a distance of about fifty yards the men in the clubhouse could clearly see the activities on the practice tee. Walter had told a bunch of the boys what was happening. Being a ham, I thought that I'd give the folks some fun. Thinking of my old friend W. C. (Bill) Fields, a terribly funny fellow whom I'd worked with on a number of occasions, I pinched some of his material and decided that this would be a good time to use it.

At first I began swinging the club without removing my heavy tweed coat. I swung the club like an old guy with gout in every joint. Stiff, tight, tense, and terrible, like some doctor friends I know down Baltimore way.

The pro tried to impart the rudiments of the golf game. With his strong, weatherbeaten hands, he showed me how to handle the club, explaining the merits of the overlapping grip, commonly known as the "Vardon grip" (which I had always used).

"What do I do now?" I asked. I wanted to laugh in the worst way, but I didn't dare. It wasn't easy to maintain a blank and goofy look on my face. After I'd got my hands reasonably right, he proceeded to place my feet in the proper position for about the tenth time. I then sprawled in a poor approximation of a golf player's stance, spreading almost the entire width of the tee.

With my feet braced wide apart, crouching down extremely low, and my behind in a most ungainly position, I expected my britches to burst asunder at any moment. When I went into that stance, I must have resembled a long-armed, big-bellied baboon bending down over the ball. I assumed various postures, all bordering on the acrobatic, and all of course with pious seriousness. Pretending complete ignorance at one point, I tried cocking my wrists and my head also in various positions until I must have looked like a clam with a broken hinge. I even cocked my knees, in keeping with the latest fad of the fair sex on the fairways nowadays.

My knees, feet, and fanny fell into the most awkward angles; no golfer ever looked so out of shape. I swung the club as though I had rubber hips, arms, shoulders. The ground seemed to quiver as I belted at the ball unmercifully. My terrible attempts at learning to swing the club were as clumsy and grotesque as a sword swallower during a spasm of hiccoughs. I kept floundering around like a drunk after a large night. Actually I believe the pro really thought that I was a bit "that way." Doubtless he had never witnessed such a sorry attempt in all his days.

So again hands, feet, shoulders, knees, hips, and elbows were all moving in wrong directions with no two parts in place or in unison. I looked like an infuriated palm tree during a Florida hurricane, or maybe as though I was frantically warding off a swarm of bees. As my teacher instructed me how to stand, the correct grip, and other basic essentials, I badly bumbled every attempt to follow his instruction. When he arranged my feet, my grip would go haywire; and by the time he had corrected my hands, my stance would be cockeyed again, and so he shifted his attention from one to the other. My attempts to catch on were pretty pathetic. No denizen of dufferdom was ever so helpless or performed so poorly as I did that day. Seemingly I was trying hard to follow instructions, but I just couldn't manage to get my club anywhere near the ball. When I did, it was still fully a foot away from making contact. I continued to belt away, to take one hefty whack after another, but the little white pill defied me.

As the lesson neared its end, I flailed away more and more ferociously, adding vim and vigor and seemingly getting madder and madder, with perspiration pouring down my face. Finally I got myself into the damnedest position imaginable. Through my grotesque endeavors, I mauled and mutilated the turf on the tee worse than a herd of stampeding Texas longhorns; but the way I was swinging, I couldn't have belted a bull over the butt with a broom. Suddenly I did it. I managed to dribble the ball a full *two* feet. And I pretended to be "pretty proud of that one, straight down the middle, too!"

What the poor pro thought of my utter helplessness I could only surmise. Time was running out on the lesson. So I thought I'd try to add a little joy to the old man's heart before leaving, and not finish up dubbing the ball. I really wanted him to think he'd made a golfer out of me in one lesson. So, following my topped shot, I chopped one, and the next I lengthened, putting it into the air a few yards, finally stretching them farther and farther onto the fairway, asking him with each attempt, "Am I doing it right, the way you just told me, sir?"

All the while I was looking directly at the pro, never at my shot, tilting my head up, turned away from the ball, to question him full face. I was by this time hitting them full and smartly, long and strong, and I apologized to him, saying, "Gee, there's nothing to this thing now. I'm sorry for being so dumb and not catching on sooner."

All through this conversation too I was still looking at him, and he finally realized that I wasn't looking at the ball at any time! A bit surprised and shaking his finger at me, he pleaded, "But, laddie, you must keep yer head down and the eye on the ball!"

"Damn it," I answered, "I've done that all morning with you, but look what I can do this way. This is simple. I like to look at the ball and see it fly in the air. Why, it's beautiful!"

And I sailed one after another right down the fairway 250 yards while talking, and all the time the kindly gent was shaking his head with disapproval mumbling, "Amazing, amazing!"

I kept on improving and kept thanking him for his great tuition, and then I paid and double-tipped him. In parting, I commented enthusiastically, "Say, I like this so much that I'll be back in a couple of days and I'd sure appreciate it if you could pick out your best set of 'links' for me."

"Oorr now," he replied, "They're not links, laddie, they are golf clubs."

"Oh, pardon my ignorance," I insisted. "But whatever you call them, I'll be back for some, and you pick me out the best set you've got."

Now he looked at me, scratched his bristly chin, and said, "Aye, haste ye back, sonnie, haste ye back."

PART FIVE

AMUSING INCIDENTS AND TRICK SHOTS

Moments of laughter on and off the golf course were a way of life for me. They seem almost too many to enumerate, but some of my best-remembered ones might cause a chuckle still. One incident happened in Cleveland, Ohio, at the attractive Canterbury Golf Club one summer day at the height of the tournament season. I was playing an exhibition round to a very large gallery and the middle western sun was beating down on us with the air dead-still and the humidity making a sandwich of our socks and our plus fours.

As I came to the tee on a long par five hole, the spectators scattered out in front. Some positioned themselves at the green, others near the heavy rough, and the largest group down along the fairway in the vicinity of my drive's destination. I'll never forget that hole because I played a straight beauty of a shot, and there was the usual scamper ahead for a view of my next hit. It was a bit of a dog-leg, and so to make up for the routine flatness of the terrain I decided on my brassie wood for best control. Reaching for my club, I noticed out of the corner of my eye a rather attractive and

113

well-dressed woman wearing a large sun hat strolling down the fairway. Of course, I was used to the crowds, but I remember that she registered on my mind because her back was turned to me, and she wasn't watching.

Arranging my grip, then my stance, I lined up to the green. I wanted position rather than distance. When I hit the ball, it really hooked, flying disastrously down the fairway with lots of power and zing, as that shot does. It hit that prim lady low on her back, or truthfully squarely on her bottom, jarring not only her hat but her composure too. The noise was amazing. It sounded just like my ball had hit a board, making a large crack, careening and bouncing back onto the fairway. Immediately she put her arm up to shield her face and started rubbing the back of her head, covering her embarrassment about where the ball had really landed. Of course my ball was saved, but I hurried down the fairway to see how she was and whether she was hurt.

When I reached her and started to apologize, she interrupted me saying, "Oh, it was you, was it? On the way out here I got nothing but noise from my husband, back-seat driving all the way, telling me everything that I was doing wrong, and now I get to the golf course and I find another one!"

It was "back-seat driving" all right. While her husband's hurt her tranquillity, mine had surely hurt her pride, her girdle stays, and what lay beneath!

Along these same lines, in a way, is the story of my exhibition for the inmates at San Quentin Prison in California, one of the most interesting places that I've ever performed. I had given my show for all kinds of hospital patients, the maimed, and even the blind, for the armed services and even for inmates of mental hospitals—and now a high-security prison!

114

Warden Duffy was in charge then, and he made a personal request for me to come out and do a show for the boys. I'll never forget the security check that I went through before entering the prison. I had to go into an X-ray booth with my clubs to make sure that I wasn't concealing any hidden weapons. Of course, my golf gear looked a bit weird, but they passed me through, and when I arrived before the exhibition, Warden Duffy took me around to see the whole operation. Along death row to the gas chamber, he explained the prison setup and life to me. I hadn't realized that most of those fellows were long-termers, the often-convicted criminals, and that many were in for life. I must say, though, that when I arrived in the "yard," I forgot all this and saw instead just a sea of eager faces like any other crowd; more than fifteen hundred men had gathered to watch.

I found that the enclosed "yard," the size of a ball park, wasn't big enough for a full golf shot, and so I had to send the balls out over the wall. In fact, midway through the show, I started kidding my audience through my microphone saying, "I wonder if some of you boys would mind getting my balls outside there, over that high thing."

They roared with laughter. People are all the same when it comes to humor, and these men reacted to my sense of play enthusiastically. In particular, they nearly tore the place up when I started aiming my shots at the guard who was "walking the wall." Of course it was part of the prison routine for the guards to pace the road on the rampart of the wall, but they'd never been targets of golf balls before. At first I sent an occasional iron shot toward them and then increased my attack so that they were falling and ducking from my well-targeted rain of balls.

This, of course, was wonderful fun for the fellows below. So I took my cue from them and beamed a number-one iron at the chief "bull" guard. He was confused and fell over to avoid the hit and in the process dropped his rifle. While he was recovering his weapon, he made the mistake of bending over and turning his back to us, whereupon I sent my next shot directly in, to land squarely on the seat of his pants. After that maneuver, you could have heard the roar across San Francisco Bay. It must have lasted five minutes.

That more or less closed up the show, but as I was gathering my clubs to leave, several inmates came over to help me and to talk. They seemed like normal fellows, joking about their situation and not dangerous in any way. All of them wanted to help me with my bag like a bunch of young caddies, and I left them with a feeling of comradeship.

Of course, playing golf matches in unusual places was never a complete surprise to me. I remember one experience when Walter and I were playing an American tour and we startled a few fans. We had dropped down across the border to Mexico for a match at Caliente. It was a new course and surrounded by parched, arid ground. We'd finished our match and were fooling around in the locker room, remarking on the dry heat, the dust, and the contrast of the green fairways, when Walter suddenly challenged me to a match from the clubhouse door to the toilet bowl in our room back at the hotel.

The inn where we were staying was at least a mile away, and the idea struck a real funny bone in me. Harold Lloyd was with us at the time and wanted to include this "Sugar-Bowl Championship" in a forthcoming movie he was planning to make of the fun of golf. As I recall, we began to collect quite a crowd, and we decided on a friendly fifty-dollar bet, starting at the clubhouse. We set off shooting right down the driveway, past the jabbering caddies, right down the main street, with the ball bouncing from sidewalk to pavement (more than startling the local traffic), up onto the lawn by the flower beds, through the lobby of the inn, down the corridors, and finally into our room.

By this time we really had a crowd of onlookers, cheering and making side wagers of their own. In the end I won, because Walter had trouble picking his approach club off the tile floor of the bathroom. On the first try my pitching wedge picked the ball clean, and it ended the contest with a polite splash right into the white bowl.

Another time we played from a hotel fairway in Chicago. Walter and I, and our hotel was across the highway from Lincoln Park. It was rather a lazy day, and I was practicing my swing off the rug in our sitting room. Walter was sitting watching me when his gaze wandered out our window, toward the park below. He noticed a bunch of bums stretched out in the sunshine on the grass. A sly grin came over his face, and with a casual wave in the direction of the open window, he said, "Bet you couldn't land one by those rummies, Kirkie!"

Not answering him immediately, I crossed the room, raised the window the whole way, and leaned out. "See that fellow there," I pointed. "I'll put it right in his pocket."

"You'll smash the window first," he predicted.

"Oh, no" I said, "I can knock it right through there."

Standing back from the window a piece, I looked out over the sea of moving traffic to where this particular bum was stretched out by the benches. With a casual look over my shoulder, I walked over to my bag, which was propped up in the corner of the room, and grabbed my seven iron. Planting my feet not too wide and playing off my left side while keeping my arms in close to my body, I stroked the ball off the carpet, landing the shot just two feet from the old guy in the park. He heard the thud of the ball landing

117

and rose up to look around for its source. He scanned front and back, over toward some trees, but of course he couldn't spot anyone hitting. So after a quick, shifty glance, he walked over to the ball and very carefully picked it up and hid it in his pocket.

By now I had another one flying at him, and this one landed even closer. Walter was urging me on and was getting a supply of balls ready to take a shot himself. Meanwhile the confused old fellow searched the limits of the park with his eyes and even the highway, full of honking traffic. Again he bent over and picked up the second ball, by which time I had hit a third one, landing it right at his feet as he was bending down. By now he was really puzzled, and he took the balls over to a friend, who was sprawled not too far away. The two of them never figured out where this rain of balls came from, and Walter and I had a good laugh from our elevated tee!

Later that day Walter put the frosting on the cake by calling one of the local pros at the most fashionable country club in the area. Camouflaging his voice, he said that he'd heard of the pro, that he had been recommended as a great teacher, and Walter wanted to know whether he could have a lesson. The pro answered, "Well, when could you get out here?"

"Oh," replied Walter, "I can't leave here. I thought you could give me a lesson over the phone!" With the most sincere tone to his voice he confided, "I can tell you what I'm doing wrong, and I thought you could advise me how to correct it just by talking. He paused, "In fact, I'll put the phone down on the floor here and you can listen to the swish of my club. Can't you tell by that?"

Of course there were other times that we tried to kid golfers along, not using the phone. One cold night in Maine,

I remember, we were in our car and passed a driving range. I asked Walter to slow down and back up because I used to get a lot of material from watching people and their swings. Their humorous characteristics really showed up on a practice range. We pulled over and walked to a floodlit bench and watched for a while. We were both wearing heavy polo coats, and we sat there watching a chap slash away at the balls, getting nowhere. After a few minutes Hagen made some suggestion to the fellow which the man really resented. He grumbled that we probably "couldn't hit the ball any further than he could."

This tickled Walter, and so he got up and asked to borrow the fellow's club for a hit. Well, he never even took off his heavy coat—just stood up to the ball, and with that stylish swing of his he sent one thundering out a couple of hundred yards. Without a word he turned and walked back to the car while the man stood dazed.

Later that week we found ourselves driving through New Hampshire on a sunny Sunday. The leaves were turning all the bright fall colors. We had the top down on our convertible, and the countryside opened up in total beauty. We suddenly realized that we were passing a golf course that bordered a pleasant twisting road. Paralleled next to us stretched several holes, and we slowed down and then stopped to watch a foursome of older men tee off. The second man in the group was having a terrible time. He took several practice swings and nervous swats, dipped his right knee in, and lunged at the ball three times with no success!

At this point Walter let out a giggle. He just couldn't hold himself back. All four men turned to stare at us. The gent who had just goofed so badly straightened up and barked at us saying, "If you think it's so easy, try it for yourself!"

With that Walter nudged me and suggested that I get out

and "hit a few." Again we were dressed in regular clothes, not golf attire, and looked like normal tourists. I walked over to the ball, still teed up where the man had been unsuccessful in connecting with it, took the club out of the gent's hand, and made note that it was a three wood.

"Well," I said, "You can't hit a ball stuck up in the air like that!" And I took it off the big long tee and jammed it down into the damp ground. Pushed it right into the sod and stood up to it without taking a practice swing—and knocked it right down the fairway a fair piece. "That's the way to do it," I said, and walked straight back to the car.

You've never heard such a holler in your life. About this time one of the caddies had recognized Hagen sitting in the shade. Walter was such a glamourous fellow that he had a lot of admirers—of both sexes—and this young lad tagged him out of the blue. I guess the caddie told the members that he was sure it was Walter, who was supposed to be playing down the line a bit later in the week. All the men came over to the car. They proceeded to make a huge fuss over us both, inviting us to dinner and offering to make a party out of the evening.

Masquerading as a duffer or pro was never a novelty for me. I was hired many a time to be a sort of secret weapon, joke-type partner or opponent, with many business and professional groups. One time in particular the new president of the Chesapeake and Ohio Railroad was playing a match, and I was hired to be his partner. I was told to "blow it," and I spent the entire round dubbing my shots off the toe of my club between people's feet, looping shots around trees, skiing them into ponds, and generally playing a frightening game. Meanwhile, this big executive tried to coach me all the way, changing my grip and stance, giving advice of every kind and losing every bet (and he'd made plenty).

In the afternoon we were supposed to take on some other opponents. My partner started to talk his way out of playing with me. He said that he thought he had better switch, that the match had played too one-sided. And he refused me as his teammate. We resumed play, with me now opposing him. On this round I swung my shots out, hooking and slicing, topping the ball, even skipping it across a lake (as I had in the morning), but somehow always having them come to rest on the fairway. Each time I exclaimed about how "lucky" they were. And he agreed that "they really *were* lucky."

My partner and I beat him every hole on that round, and again he lost his bets, all of them. Afterward, back in the clubhouse, they told him who he had played with, but evidently he never did believe them because he claimed to know me personally. He was a boastful person and was overheard to exclaim, "Oh, I know Joe Kirkwood well, and that sure wasn't him playing! I'd recognize Kirkwood anywhere!"

My trick-shot training actually helped me a few times during tournament play. One incident comes immediately to mind. It happened on the fourteenth hole at the Forest Hill Field Club during the first round of the Hale America Sectional Trials. I'd hooked my drive to a bunker on the left side of the fairway, and the ball lay in some deep grass on the trap bank. To address it I had to take an awkward stance with only one foot on the ground. Such a stance is even more difficult if you can't get balance with your rear foot grounded, using it as an anchor for your swing. However, in this case the reverse was true, and I had no choice but to place all my weight on the right foot. All I knew was that from my storklike position I had to keep the clubhead traveling in a flat trajectory. This circus shot came off per-

121

fectly, the ball covering 230 yards en route to the green's edge. I finished the 480-yard hole with a birdie four.

Then there was a recovery that I made from under a wire fence on the ninth hole at Inwood during the 1923 National Open. It never could have been executed by anybody but a stunt shooter. My drive had lodged under the steel-mesh barrier separating the fairway from the road. To reach the ball I had to climb the fence. Taking a mashie niblick, I turned the blade upside down, addressed the ball left-handed, and hit a low flying shot that reached the green 150 yards away. Because of the outward incline of the top strands of the barbed wire, I couldn't climb over the fence from my position outside the course. While I was wondering how to get back on the course again, a taxicab rumbled down the road. Hailing the driver, I climbed in and rode a quarter of a mile back to the entrance gate. No other golfer has ever taken a taxi ride between strokes in an open championship.

However, my normal pattern was to play my matches straight—that is, to win. But once the tension was over and the match in the bag, I'd give the gallery folks a deserved bit of fun. I recall a typical contest played in Calcutta, India, when on the seventeenth hole it was all sewed up and in our pockets. Just before the green, my ball lay in some longish grass, squarely in line with the pin. All I had to do was chip it in close, but instead I called over to Walter to take a look. "We're right near our balcony of the Grand Hotel!" I said.

At this point, our caddie scowled at me in annoyance. Turning my back away from the hole, I took out my wedge and swung through. To the amazement of the uncomprehending crowd, the ball made a complete arc behind and around a belt of trees and bounced over some rhododendron bushes onto the green, finishing a yard from the pin.

Perhaps the final tribute to one of these blind loop shots with backstop happened down Texas way, where they placed a tablet on a tree to commemorate a play. In this case I'd found my ball behind a tree, stymied for a direct pitch to the green. The crowd thought that I would chip to safety, but it seemed a wasted stroke. So I hit the ball right across a river (they thought the ball would surely end in a watery grave), but it hooked around, circling like a boomerang, finishing on the green, where I holed out for a birdie three.

It could be said that these and many more moments of fun and entertainment made the complete circle of my life. For in the end, it was like the beginning—amusement and laughter for others was my guiding light.

SUCKER

I delighted in the kind of deception that I stumbled upon one winter's trip that my son Ronnie and I took to Florida in 1968. You might say that we went a-fishin'.

We had driven South in a leisurely fashion and found ourselves in the Florida Keys. Following our first succulent lobster dinner, the two of us drifted over to the marina where the charter boats were tied up. The evening was a fine, calm one. Some of the captains were puttering about on deck tidying up after the day's catch. Others were just coming in from their cruises, and they all had elaborate boats.

We got down to the end of the line to find one beauty that hadn't been out. The captain in the back of the boat was swinging a golf club. Surprised, I said to him, "Got a pretty good swing there, fellow."

He answered, "Yes, I play quite a bit. Like golf better than I do fishing."

"You weren't out there today, were you?" I asked.

"Nope," he said, and looked out to sea.

Picking up the conversation again, I commented, "We were interested in a fishing trip, some deep-sea stuff."

"Well," he replied, "You made a remark about my golf swing. You play golf?"

"Oh, yes," I said. "I play a little."

He paused some and then questioned, "Maybe you'd be interested—I have a deal. I play anybody a round of golf, and if they beat me, they get a free ride—a free trip in the boat."

"That sounds pretty good. You must be a fair golf player," I answered.

He smiled a cocky one saying, "I'm a four handicap."

"Well," I said, "That's exceptionally good," and I didn't talk further, just ambled down away.

When I got about two boats along, I overheard him call to one of the other skippers, "Boy, Mac—I think I've got a sucker!"

Well, I didn't go back right away, but after a while I did return and started up with him again. "Look," I said, "I've been thinking that deal of yours over, whereby if I happen to beat you in golf, I get a free boat ride; and if you beat me, I pay double." Hesitating, I asked, "What's your fee?"

"Oh," he said, "A hundred dollars for the day."

I scratched my head and thought a minute more and asked him, "Well, when can you play golf?"

Quick as lightning, he answered, "Not before nine o'clock tomorrow morning!"

The next day dawned sunny and smooth, and I found the little nine-hole course all right. It was a short layout, just up my alley, for I'd been playing a lot of golf that winter, and I was right on beam.

I arrived out there with only three clubs in my hand. The

captain had a proper bagful, like a pro. With some curiosity he asked me, "Where are your clubs?"

"Well," I answered, "here they are. There's no caddies around, and I don't want to lug a big bag about. I think I'll get by pretty well with these three clubs."

"OK, suit yourself," he said, intimating that it was a big joke that all I had was three clubs.

"Want to play the back tees or the short tees?" he asked.

"Oh, whichever way you want to play," I answered, and he chose the back tees.

Striding ahead, he was the first to hit, and he sliced it right off the tee. It wasn't a good shot at all and landed in the rough. I stepped up and threw my ball on the ground, not even teeing it up. With a quick glance forward, I took out my four wood and played a large hook, circled it way out over the palmettos, and brought it back on the fairway. Looking up, I squinted and said, "Kinda windy up there. Must be a high wind."

After a few holes went by, he started to stare at me. I found that he wasn't as good as he said he was. And he was getting confused as I sunk six- and eight-foot putts with my five iron. I stayed just ahead of him, but hooked and sliced around traps and palm scrub as I went, beating him just one up on the last hole.

We won that free boat ride for the next day, and we did enjoy ourselves. Ronnie and I had good luck and a grand time. After we were in that evening and saying our good-bys, our captain couldn't contain himself.

"You wouldn't want to try the same thing again?" he said. He wasn't satisfied and thought that I'd just been lucky.

I hesitated and then replied, "Yes, I'll take on your deal for another round."

The next day we repeated, playing eighteen, but this time

I threw a bunch of birdies at him, beat him pretty badly, and he couldn't understand it. We earned another boat ride (at a hundred dollars a day), and at the end of this one I tried to thank him for all the fun we'd had. I told him we'd never thought we could have such good times so far from home. After dinner I shook his hand for the last time, saying, "Look, if you ever come to Vermont, don't fail to come to Stowe. I live up there, and we have a nice golf course."

Then I handed him my card. He still didn't know who I was, of course. He took my card and looked at it, and then slowly at me, cocked his head to the side and said, "You're not *the* Joe Kirkwood, the golfer?"

"Oh," I said, "I've played a bit in my time."

"Well," he debated, "I thought the first day we were out that you were just dumb lucky, hooking and slicing around trees and things like that."

Hands in pocket and smiling I answered, "I really came down to fish, not to golf."

But still looking at me, up, down, and sideways, he took the card over to the captain in the next boat and showed it to him. You've never heard such a roar in your life. They were waiting for him to get trapped. He'd been getting away with this stuff for quite a long while, and this time he was hooked.

Leaving I said to him, "Listen, friend, I'll be back again, and maybe we'll go out and have some more fishing, but meanwhile I'd be careful how you use that word 'sucker.'"

LEO DIEGAL'S FUNERAL

Leo Diegal, the famous American golfing pro, was a close buddy of Walter Hagen's and mine. In fact, we were neighbors in the same apartment building. Jerico Manor, in Philadelphia for a time. Leo was a man who lived and played hard. He was a heavy smoker, and it was this that eventually brought about his end, when he developed a serious case of lung cancer.

Before his passing—I guess in an attempt to regain his health—he moved to California where we lost track of him. He died out West, and by chance I read about it in the *Philadelphia Inquirer.* The obituary mentioned that he was to be buried the next day in Detroit, his home town, and so, with apologies to my wife, I left by car the same day, alerting Hagen that we should attend the funeral together.

When I reached the athletic club in Detroit where Walter had rooms, at nine o'clock the following morning, the Haig was just coming in. He had been out all night on a binge and was feeling no pain or shame. I did my best to bring him around, got him into a cold shower, and after some breakfast said, "Where do we go to say our last farewells to Leo? What church are they holding the service in?"

"Oh," he answered, "I've got it all written down on a piece of paper over on the bureau. Grab that, and we'll drive over in my new car."

Of course he knew that he wasn't in good shape, and so he agreed to let me do the driving. We found our way across town to the church that Hagen had noted, and, naturally, we arrived late. Always late with Hagen, never on time—I called him "the late Walter Hagen."

When we reached the church, we found it crowded with people. It was difficult to park the car, but we finally managed and found our way inside. By now everybody was seated, and the only remaining space was on a bench at the very rear of the building. We found ourselves involved in a Roman Catholic funeral mass complete with Latin liturgy, and frequent kneeling and praying. Friend Walter wasn't quite up to it all. While he was slumping and snoring and the priest was saying the mass, I took a good look around and thought to myself, "That's funny. I don't recognize anybody—nobody looks even familiar!"

Along about then I was busy prodding Walter, keeping him from keeling over onto my shoulder, while his noises were growing louder and more baritone (I was sure they were reaching up to the belfry). Straightening up, I shook him and questioned, "Walter, are you sure we're at the right funeral?"

"Oh, yes," he said. "Hush, keep quiet! You're disturbing the people."

Somehow I wasn't satisfied that we were in the correct place, but all the ushers were positioned at the doors, and I could only speculate.

We suffered through some of the service, but the more

129

I looked around, the more convinced I became that there had been an error. When it was nearly over, I managed to work my way over to one of the attendants and whispered to him, "Pardon me, my good man, but are we at Leo Diegal's funeral?"

"Who?" he said. "Who did you say?"

Now it was affirmed. We were in the wrong church. I squirmed my way back to Walter, who was now fast asleep. His snores had developed a whistle at the end of the exhalation, making him that much more audible. When I reached him, I shook him awake, and his reaction was immediate.

"At the wrong funeral! What the hell! Oh, *no.*"

Up we got and started to squeeze past the seated throng. Suddenly he faltered and landed with a thud, tripping over an old lady's leg. Using her as a lever, he started to rise. To put it mildly, she was indignant. And as much as Walter tried to apologize, she tried to wave him off and finally commanded, "I accept your apology, but, young man, let go of my leg!"

Many a snicker was quieted on that one. Meanwhile I found the undertaker and got him aside to try and see whether he knew where Diegal's funeral was being held. Fortunately, he had the correct address.

Armed with the proper information, off we started again. By this time we were really running late and found that we had to go six miles or more to another suburb, difficult to find by nonnatives like us. When we finally did reach our destination, the congregation was filing out of the church and heading for their cars to go to the cemetery. This time, at least, there were many familiar faces, and we followed the cars to the graveside.

Even after all this maneuvering, it became apparent to me that Hagen was still relaxed. He wasn't feeling any pain, and try as I would, nothing would subdue a certain enthusiasm in him. I managed to keep him fairly quiet, and after the service was over and I was steering him toward the car, he stopped firmly in his tracks, saying, "Kirkie, are you in any hurry?"

"No," I said. "I came up here for Leo's funeral, and we've missed most of it, but I'm not in any hurry."

"Well," he confided, "let's wait a minute." And he kept looking furtively back toward the grave until the last mourner was gone and we were quite alone. Then he ambled back.

"There's something I wanted to say to Leo," he smiled at me. "But hold on a minute and you stand right here and wait. I'll be directly back."

At which point Hagen made a very sober jog to our car, by now managing to stand alone.

Out of the trunk of the vehicle he produced a six-pack of beer and sauntered gleefully back to where I was standing and then positioned himself at the head of the coffin. With a nod toward me, he opened three bottles and put his arm across the casket.

"Leo," he said, "I couldn't leave you this way without wishing you a personal farewell. We've been together many years, been buddies all that time, played a lot of golf, and had a lot of laughs together and a lot of beers together."

For perhaps twenty minutes I stood by while Walter talked to Leo as if they were side by side in the locker room, reminiscing about all the games and tournaments we'd shared among us. He'd tap on the casket and laugh and smile at me, and I couldn't help but marvel at the man's memory—not one bit clouded now, just as vivid as the times we'd spent together. Suddenly it dawned on me that this was a tremendous attitude to take toward somebody who had passed away. Walter showed every emotion that a man could show. He had humor and kindness, some longing, but never any sadness, and his final comments were that he just wanted to share these beers for the long trip ahead.

"And by the way," he questioned, "how the blazes did they get you in there with those elbows?"

They had buried Leo with his lucky putter, one that I'd given him and that had become his charmed club. He won many tournaments with that stick and it was in the coffin with him. His style of putting, I might add, was famous too, kind of chicken-on-the-wing, with elbows crooked outward.

"May you and your putter rust in peace," Walter said. And he put his arm around my shoulder and said, "Come on, Kirkie, that's it."

"TRAVELS"

I've had my laughs where tall giraffes
laid stymies from the tee.
I've missed my two's where kangaroos
were standing close by me.

From Burma to the Golden Gate,
from Maine to Singapore,
from Sydney to the Great Divide,
I've stood and hollered, "Fore."

The Seven Seas have known my tees,
beneath an all-world sky.
I've carried ruts and missed my putts
where cobras slithered by.

From Palm Beach to the Chinese Wall,
by Durban's Tropic Loam,
I've slashed my drives along the route,
from California up to Nome.

I've made my score in old Jahore,
cheered by Sultanic queens,
where tigers glared and rhinos stared,
and pythons trapped the greens.

From Shanghai to the Río Grande,
by Amazon and Nile,
I haven't tried Moscow yet,
but that can wait awhile.

JOE KIRKWOOD

APPENDICES

1. TEACHING TIPS

Nobody should begin building a house without plans and blueprints. Nor should anybody begin learning golf without first acquiring a firm foundation in the essential fundamentals, the basic principles of the game.

A good golf game is an acquired art, not a gift, as many folks are led to believe. Actually, the expression "gift" was merely an old Scottish adage, invented by another clansman, resorted to mainly as a means of enticing and inveigling other Scotsmen out of their lairs to partake of a wee game of golf on the moors among the heather. And so the legend of "gift" and "golf" goes. When other canny Scotsmen learned that golf was a gift, they immediately adopted it as their national pastime.

Relax, relax, relax! After extensive study and experimenting, I find relaxation plays a very important part in the development of a hoped-for, sound, long-lived golf game. It also plays a major role in all sorts of competitive games and sports. In fact, relaxation is a vital factor in life itself. Keep it simple, keep it natural, use common sense; it's the secret of a good golf game. Take what you've got and try and improve on it, in keeping with your particular physical build and makeup. Don't try to imitate other players. It won't work, and usually it's too late.

The grip should always be the same. First shake hands with your club normally, naturally, and comfortably. Hold it gently but firmly. Too tight hands lead to tension and tend to choke; they slow and deaden all movements of the swing, killing rhythm, smoothness, and timing. Also, a tight grip shortens the swing, resulting in a loss of distance, often a chronic slice or, worse, a shank.

When addressing the ball, stand almost straight, sitting back slightly on your heels. Many stoop down to the shot and then when they top it, they think they "looked up." They didn't: they raised their bodies to get into hitting position. Stand straight, and you'll already be there.

Extend hands, arms, and club out straight. That is, don't drop your hands as though putting them in your lap.

Stand well behind the ball if you want it to go high. Turn the club face open.

Avoid swaying as you pivot. Keep your head as fixed as possible without strain. Take the club head straight back along the ground for a few inches and, as you pivot, bring the left shoulder way under. Break the wrists at the top of the swing.

Get the biggest arc possible, swing with a slow backswing and a slight hesitation at the top. Reach for the heavens with your hands, not only on the top of the backswing but also at the finish of the follow through.

Imagine that you are looking *underneath* the ball.

Whatever you do, don't let your body get ahead of your hands and club. Avoid closing the club face.

Don't fight the wind. Use the wind for extra distance whenever you are able.

In pitch and chip shots keep your arms stiff. Arms, hands, and club should all be one piece. Make it a slow, easy, rhythmical stroke with follow through.

Don't snap at it. Always avoid snapping at the ball. With your woods, avoid lunging. Keep it smooth, poetry in motion. Missing shots from picking up the club abruptly in the back swing stems from bending the left knee forward, therefore, bend this knee *inward*. Try it.

In the rough and in a bad lie open the club face to cut through the trouble.

In getting out of traps, spank the sand with the club head. Use a light touch and an easy stroke. Don't bang at it. After rain or in any hard sand, use a still lighter touch. Easy does it, caress it.

Show me a man with his head down and his feet clamped firmly on the ground, and I'll show you a man with a horrible slice. I believe that the head should be kept fairly still throughout the swing, but not necessarily "down." It's a good thing for the head to move in keeping with the body action, laterally.

Follow through. It's the same principle with every club in your bag, from the putter all the way up to the driver. The hands, arms, and club must travel as far as possible on the line of flight to obtain sound, safe, and solid results. Simply make an effort to throw your hands down the fairway in the general direction of the green. Conceive of yourself casting, curling, bowling, pitching a baseball, or even using a billiard cue. The action of follow-through is vital.

The essence, the secret that unlocks the golf swing can be summed up in three words: *relaxation, balance,* and a full *follow through*. Practice this diligently, and let the divots land where they may.

2. HIGHLIGHTS OF LIFE

Joe Kirkwood
Date of birth: April 3, 1897, Sydney, Australia
Turned professional: 1920
Date of death: October 29, 1970, Stowe, Vermont

HIGHLIGHTS

Winner: Australian Open, 1920; New Zealand Open, 1920;
Lossiemouth Tournament, 1922; Canadian Open, 1922,
1933; North and South Open, 1922, 1933; Illinois Open
Championship, 1923; California Open, 1923; Texas Open,
1923
Runner-up: Gleneagles £1,000 Tournament, 1921
Tied for Third: British Open, 1927

RECORD

1920   Winner, Australian Open
        Winner, New Zealand Championship

1921 Finalist, Gleneagles £1,000 Tournament
      Tied sixth, British Open
1922 Winner, Lossiemouth Tournament
      Winner, Canadian Open
      Winner, North and South Open
1923 Quarter-Finalist, Gleneagles £1,000 Tournament
      Fourth, British Open
      Winner, Illinois Open Championship
      Winner, California Open
      Winner, Texas Open
1926 A member of the team of American professionals who
      traveled to the British Isles to play a team of British
      professionals in a match, the forerunner of the Ryder
      Cup Matches.
1927 Tied third, British Open
1933 Winner, Canadian Open
      Winner, North and South Open